PENGUIN VEER

# BIPIN

Rachna Bisht Rawat is the author of seven books by Penguin Random House India, including the bestsellers *The Brave* and *Kargil*. She lives in Gurgaon with Hukum, the bright-eyed, bushy-tailed golden retriever; an eclectic collection of books and music; and Col. Manoj Rawat, the man in olive green, who met her when he was a gentleman cadet at the Indian Military Academy and offered to be her comrade for life. Occasionally, they are visited by Saransh the wise, who has moved out to explore the world on his own.

She can be reached at rachnabisht@gmail.com. Her Instagram handle is @rachna_bishtrawat.

## PRAISE FOR THE BOOK

'The book is a powerful narration of the life and times of General Bipin Rawat, the man in and out of uniform. A strict disciplinarian in office, he was equally warm-hearted and sociable out of it. This chronicle of memories is a poignant reminder of the collective loss that the nation and the services suffered on that fateful day of December 2021'—**General M.M. Naravane (retired), 28th Chief of the Army Staff**

'Writing an objective biography of a person who has held sensitive public appointments and a person known to you is most difficult. It is difficult to remain objective, bringing out the true character, shortcomings, achievements and failures of the subject. In *Bipin: The Man behind the Uniform*, Rachna has done a brilliant job. With her deep research, and many interviews with relations, friends and associates of Bipin Rawat, she brings out an interesting, most objective life story of India's first Chief of Defence Staff. Her eye for detail and ability to catch and describe the emotions of her interviewees is remarkable. Rachna is a master storyteller on military life. The book is a racy narrative . . . Very, very readable!'—**General V.P. Malik, former Chief of the Army Staff**

'A riveting story on the life of General Bipin Rawat, from the inspiring pen of Rachna Bisht, that makes me wonder whether "destiny is a matter of choice or a matter of chance". General Bipin Rawat believed in doing what is right, irrespective of the consequences, and that, to me, is the message of his life. A must-read for every citizen of India and the world'—**Maj. Gen. Ian Cardozo, AVSM, SM**

# BIPIN

## THE MAN BEHIND THE UNIFORM

Rachna Bisht Rawat

**PENGUIN**

**VEER**

An imprint of Penguin Random House

PENGUIN VEER

USA | Canada | UK | Ireland | Australia
New Zealand | India | South Africa | China | Singapore

Penguin Veer is an imprint of the Penguin Random House group of companies
whose addresses can be found at global.penguinrandomhouse.com

Published by Penguin Random House India Pvt. Ltd
4th Floor, Capital Tower 1, MG Road,
Gurugram 122 002, Haryana, India

First published in Penguin Veer by Penguin Random House India 2023
This edition published in 2025

ISBN 9780143472421

Typeset in Adobe Garamond Pro by Manipal Technologies Limited, Manipal

Printed at Repro India Limited

www.penguin.co.in

This is a legitimate digitally printed version of the book and therefore might not
have certain extra finishing on the cover.

*For all those serving in the armed forces and those yet to join,*
*so that you may know your first Chief of Defence Staff better*

*In early 1978, a slim and medium-built Gentleman Cadet at the Indian Military Academy, whom no one had noticed before, was being brutally thrashed by his much stronger opponent in the boxing ring. Bleeding profusely from the nose and mouth, bout after bout, he refused to give up and eventually went on to win. Surprised spectators wanted to know who the boy was. It was the shy and reticent Gentleman Cadet Bipin Rawat, of Zojila Company, who went on to become India's first Chief of Defence Staff.*
*This is his story.*

# Contents

*Foreword: Salutations, Dear Friends, Bipin and Madhu . . .*    xi

*Introduction*    xv

*Prologue*    xix

1. 'Chal, Chhotu, Bhaag!'    1
2. 'Hello! My Name Is Bipin. Can I Sit Next to You?'    15
3. The Pretty New Class Teacher    23
4. A Chopper Crash He Survived    29
5. 'Hum Sab Fauj Mein Jayenge'    39
6. Bipin Joins the NDA    43
7. Bloody-Nosed in the IMA Boxing Ring    47
8. Ayo Gorkhali!    61
9. The Bachelor with Gentle Brown Eyes    69
10. Like Father, Like Son    77
11. 'I'm Here with a Marriage Proposal'    85
12. Dancing on a Plastered Leg, under the Enemy's Nose    93

13. 'Zyada Peene Se Sehat Kharab Hoti Hai'                         99
14. Standing Up for His Battalion Commander                       107
15. 'Unrest Was at Its Peak When He Came to Congo'                113
16. A Man in a Hurry                                              121
17. A Reluctant Colonel Commandant                                129
18. Not a Man to Take Things Lying Down                           133
19. A General Who Stood by His Men                                143
20. When a Soldier Asked the Army Chief to Prove His Identity    149
21. 'Impress Me with Work, Not Gifts'                             153
22. 'He Was Garhwal's Hope for a Better Future'                   163
23. 'My Father Was a Simple Man'                                  173
24. 'Sahab Ko Toh Aaj Hero Ban Ke Hi Jana Hai'                    181
25. 'Hum Ja Rahe Hain, Beta': Tarini's Last Memory                191

Epilogue                                                          197
A Few Good Men                                                    199
Acknowledgements                                                  205

# Foreword

## Salutations, Dear Friends, Bipin and Madhu . . .

As crystal a memory can be, on 4 December 2021, in 5/11 Gorkha Rifles at Shanker Vihar, Bipin, Madhu, Payal and I were foreseeing ourselves sitting on rocking chairs next to a bonfire in Dehradun in our twilight years. It was not to be! On that fateful day, Madhu (though many of her friends called her Maddy, I could never do so) sent a picture with the unit Subedar Major on WhatsApp, saying, 'Will call you in the evening.' That evening was not to come. There were plans and plans that went a-begging.

There are memories and memories, some so trivial that they do not merit recounting! At exercises, Utpal Roy, Durgaprasad, Bipin and I invariably carried 'lotas' together for morning calls. Unimaginable today. I recollect that while doing pre-course training of 81 mm Mortars in 9 DOGRA, in US Club, Colaba, we suddenly heard the renowned baritone of Raaj Kumar, the famous actor, who was playing golf there. We asked the NCO instructor permission to go and shake hands with the actor. The instructor was so annoyed that he made us both lift up a base plate each and go around the green on which Raaj Kumar was putting. The actor saw us and gave a hearty laugh, and we were embarrassed like hell! Of course, we shook hands, and he obliged us by saying 'jaani' in his inimitable way.

Indeed, Bipin and I had differences, and some discussions sounded as if on the warpath! We differed and agreed in equal measure, discussed every known issue or personality threadbare. That was the strength of our relationship, always. It was a relationship that cannot have a suitable adjective!

We visited each other at all our postings and at homes. Gen. and Mrs Lakshman Rawat were blessed to have Bipin and Madhu looking after them through their lives so well, at Arun Vihar, Noida. I recall Gen. Lakshman Rawat at the Flag Staff House at Baramulla, when Bipin was commanding the Division; this was the same house that Gen. Lakshman Rawat had occupied in the early '80s.

I have not seen in my life the kind of recognition that Bipin and Madhu got in their demise, at 3 Kamraj Road, with swelling crowds, serpentine queues of the public at large, and people running along the cortège to Brar Square for the last rites. The Delhi–Haridwar road was lined with people with flowers as we were on our way with the last remains. And Haridwar itself! Such recognition comes to the 'rarest of the rare', and I recollect writing that phrase in the only confidential report that I had the greatest of privilege writing on Bipin, as my Second-in-Command.

Rachna Bisht Rawat has been most persuasive and forceful in putting together the life of Bipin, in her inimitable way. When we first met, I recollect mentioning to her, 'Do justice to my dearest friends. Anything short of that will be unacceptable to me!' The outcome is an eminently readable book; the best compliment is that the first read moistened my eyes.

Bipin and Madhu went so early, leaving indelible memories. So long, dear friends, till we meet again.

**Lt Gen. Rakesh Sharma**
Former Adjutant-General
Gen. Bipin Rawat Chair of Excellence, USI
Distinguished Fellow, Vivekananda International Foundation

# Introduction

In August 2019, when the nation was commemorating the twentieth anniversary of Operation Vijay, popularly known as the Kargil war, I went to the South Block, Central Secretariat, at Raisina Hill in Delhi, to gift the then Chief of Army Staff, General Bipin Rawat, a copy of my book *Kargil*.

Accompanied by my editor Gurveen Chadha and son, Saransh, I stood in the meeting room, with all the previous Chiefs of the Indian Army looking down at me—stately and dignified, each one of them capable of making authors nervous with their gaze, even if it only came from a portrait on the wall. Two beautiful paintings—marking India's two historic war victories, 1971 and Kargil—adorned facing walls. We were still looking around when the General walked in, perfectly on time, looking distinguished in his olive-green uniform.

Casual and smiling, he reached out to shake hands with me, with Gurveen and with Saransh, who was then a rebellious teenager and had absolutely refused to get his long hair cut for this meeting, despite repeated calls from his Army officer dad to do so. Manoj was posted in Allahabad those days and was horrified by the thought of his son going to meet his Chief with untidy hair.

I apologized to Gen. Rawat for Saransh's hair, but he just looked at Saransh and inquired, 'Do you want to join the Army, young man?'

'No, sir. I want to be a commercial pilot.'

This from a boy who belongs to a family that has given generations of soldiers. I cringed.

But Gen. Rawat's smile stayed as warm. 'That is perfectly fine. Not everybody needs to join the Army or keep their hair short. All the best to you,' he said, winning over a teenage fan right away.

We had been told that the Chief was following a very tight schedule and could give us just ten minutes, which should be enough for a quick photo shoot, where he would accept a copy of the book from me. Not only did he do that, but he also helpfully suggested that we stand under the painting of soldiers hoisting the national flag on a captured peak in Kargil; and he sat down next to me, looking relaxed and unhurried as he asked questions about the book and the people I had interviewed.

Since he appeared so approachable, I asked him to verify a story I had heard about him: about how he had recently been stopped by a young soldier on guard duty in the cantonment (when he had been driving his own car) and asked to show his ID card. He laughed and assured me it was true, and added, 'He was just doing his job. And doing it well.'

He then told us about a helicopter crash he had survived in Dimapur: the helicopter he was travelling in as Corps Commander had developed a snag and crashed soon after lifting off. He said that all he had suffered were a few cuts and bruises. All those present in the room that day marvelled at the story of his miraculous escape. 'It was the grace of god,' he said, and, waiting courteously for me to finish my tea, wished me luck and left.

I did not know Gen. Rawat much then, but I had liked him a lot. He came across as earthy, straightforward and a genuinely nice person. No one had any inkling then that he would go on to become India's first Chief of Defence Staff or that we would lose him in a tragic helicopter accident just two years later. Not in my wildest dreams had I thought that I would be writing his biography. But that was destined to happen.

When I started writing *Bipin: The Man Behind the Uniform*, I slowly got to know the COAS I had once had tea with a little better. It was while interviewing Lt Col B.K. Singh (retd), who had piloted the chopper that had crashed in Dimapur, that I learnt that Gen. Rawat had climbed out of the badly mangled Cheetah with a bloodstained shirt and had assured Singh, 'Just don't worry! These things happen. You did your best.' He had then asked for another helicopter and done the trip a few hours later, completely unaffected by the crash.

As you read this book you will come across many heart-warming episodes from the life of India's highest-ranking defence officer, whom most of us saw only in uniform. And though I am aware of the extreme emotions he stirred in people, many of them in uniform, he was indeed a remarkable man. He lived by his beliefs, took up stands for the army that many others in his position might not have taken, since they would be considered diplomatically incorrect; and he had the moral courage to stand by what he had said, face criticism and take responsibility when it was due.

Gen. Bipin Rawat was a simple man. When he was young, he was quiet and reticent, never mentioning to anyone that his father was a General. He would always carry his own luggage, even when he went home. When he rose to the highest rank, he liked watching musical talent shows on television. He sometimes went to sleep sharing his bed with his dogs. He didn't care much about what he was wearing. His clothes were mostly bought by his buddies or by his wife. He was often ribbed by friends who told him that he had the hide of a rhino, at which he would just laugh. He insisted his daughters would use public transport, and not an official army vehicle, even when he was COAS.

I would like to request his strongest critics to read this book. They will then realize that he lived his life by the same rules that he applied to others. He might have had his flaws—and who doesn't?—but the fact is that he was honest, straightforward, kind and a nationalist who believed in doing what he felt was right for his country. Which is more than what can be said for a lot of other people.

To those who loved him, I would like to say I hope this book tells you at least some stories that you didn't know and brings him back to life again, if only for a while. If that happens, I will be satisfied that my efforts have not gone to waste.

# Prologue

## Radio Silence

8 December 2021
Sulur Air Force Station, Tamil Nadu
Around 11.35 a.m.

It is a clear winter day. The sun shines brightly. A pleasant breeze rustles the leaves of the coconut trees. A fixed-wing Indian Air Force Embraer aircraft has landed on the main runway and is taxiing down to the VIP Reception Tarmac. It has come from the Palam air base, Delhi, covering a distance of 1951 km in about two and a half hours. When it finally comes to a standstill in Parking Bay Number 1, the pilot quickly disembarks and stands by the stepladder to receive the VIP guest he has flown. Group Captain Varun Singh, Shaurya Chakra, Directing Staff, Defence Services Staff College (DSSC), who has come to Sulur to escort his special guests back to Wellington, also stands beside him.

General Bipin Rawat, Param Vishisht Seva Medal, Uttam
Yudh Seva Medal, Ati Vishisht Seva Medal, Vishisht Seva Medal,
Sena Medal and Yudh Seva Medal, Chief of Defence Staff, has
emerged at the door of the aircraft. All those waiting come to
attention and salute as the highest-ranking officer in the Indian
armed forces walks down the stepladder in his crisp uniform, his
eyes bright and alert. Mrs Madhulika Rawat walks behind him.
She is dressed in a deep blue salwar kameez and has a warm smile
on her face.

The others in the four-star General's entourage follow. These
include his Defence Assistant, Brigadier Lakhbinder Singh Lidder,
Staff Officer Lt Col Harjinder Singh, Administration NCO Havildar
Satpal Rai and Personal Security Officers Naik Gursewak Singh,
Naik Jitender Kumar, Lance Naik B. Sai Teja and Lance Naik Vivek
Kumar. All four are para commandos.

In Parking Bay 2, just a few yards away, stands a stocky Mi-17
V5 helicopter with its auxiliary engine humming. Wing Commander
P.S. Chauhan, Commanding Officer of the 109 Helicopter Unit (the
Knights), located at Sulur Air Force Station, waits beside it. He is an
experienced pilot who has flown the route frequently on VIP as well
as training sorties. His co-pilot, Squadron Leader Kuldeep Singh, is
already seated inside the chopper along with the flight crew, which
includes flight gunner Junior Warrant Officer Rana Pratap Das and
flight engineer Junior Warrant Officer (JWO) Pradeep. They are
all relaxed and ready for the flight. At Sulur, pilots do the Coonoor
route so many times that they refer to it as the 'milk run', a World
War II term used to describe a regular trip during which nothing
unusual tends to happen.

Chauhan steps forward and introduces himself to the CDS, who
shakes his hand warmly. He then boards the chopper, accompanied
by Madhulika and his staff officers. Chauhan enters the cockpit. The
flight gunner pulls up the ladder. Co-pilot Kuldeep starts reading
from the cockpit checklist. Chauhan switches on the chopper's two
main engines. The rotors swirl into action, and the deafening roar of

the motor fills up the helicopter. Madhulika looks at her husband, who nods back reassuringly.

By the side of the chopper stands the marshal with two batons in his hands, guiding the lift-off. The Mi-17 starts taxiing to the runway. The pilot pulls the joystick forward, making the chopper's nose dip down. He then opens the throttle. At about 11.48 a.m., pilot lifts the chopper into a steady hover and then eases the cyclic stick forward to achieve perfect take off altitude. The chopper starts gaining altitude and departs smoothly on the desired climb path carrying ten passengers and four crew members on board.

* * *

The officers present there, to see the CDS off, stand at attention as the strong draft from the Mi-17's powerful rotors makes their clothes whip against their bodies. They watch as it makes a beautiful copybook take-off towards Wellington, where it is scheduled to land at the Wellington Gymkhana Club helipad. The General is on a visit to the Defence Services Staff College (DSSC) to address the faculty and student officers of the Staff Course.

The chopper crosses Coimbatore city and then soars high. Brig. Lakhbinder is reading a WhatsApp message from his wife, Geetika. 'Enjoy Wellington! It has given us so much,' she has written. Lakhbinder smiles and types out a reply. Harjinder is resting his head back on the seat. The face of his thirteen-year-old daughter, Preet, flashes before his eyes. She has been the biggest gift of his life. He takes a deep breath and closes his eyes. Satpal Rai's mind is in Darjeeling and on his wife with a smile brighter than the green *pothe ki mala* she wears. She has spent her life waiting for him. This time he will take her on that long-overdue vacation, he promises himself. Bipin and Madhulika, who have done the flight before, are looking out of the window, enjoying the pristine view.

The chopper flies for nearly forty minutes, crossing tea gardens and thick forests. Bipin points out the Mettupalayam railway station to Madhu. This is where the toy train to Ooty starts. It covers a forty-six-kilometre track that runs through the picturesque Nilgiri mountains. He knows that Wellington should now be just about ten minutes away.

It is then that they both notice the clouds swirling in from over the hills. The chopper is soon surrounded by a dense grey mist that blocks their view completely. The two pilots speak to each other. They are convinced that the helicopter should be above Wellington, but visibility is zero. They don't realize that they have strayed about 10 km from their route and are flying above steep hills. The passengers peer blindly into the thick clouds through their windows. They are a little confused but not unduly worried.

Suddenly there is a deadly crash. and raging flames engulf the Mi-17. And then there is complete radio silence.

*Interviews with family members and creative licence have been used to recreate General Bipin Rawat's last chopper flight from Sulur. Landing time for the Embraer has been approximated from the time the chopper took off from Sulur Air Force Station, which has been stated as 11.45 a.m.*

*8 December 2021*
*Nilgiris, Tamil Nadu*
*Around 12.14 p.m.*

*Coimbatore-based wedding photographer Joe Paul, fifty-two, his friend Nazar and some members from Nazar's family are on a day trip to a place called Runnymede, near Ooty, for a family photo shoot. Parking their Ford EcoSport on the road, they enter the lush green forested area and are walking along the railway track when they are startled by the deep reverberating hum of a chopper. It is flying directly overhead.*

*Fascinated by the helicopter's close proximity, Joe takes out his cell and starts making a video. Suddenly a swirling cloud of dense mist appears in the sky. Even as the horrified onlookers watch, the helicopter flies into the fog and slowly disappears. Soon after, they hear the sound of rotors scraping the branches of trees and then a loud echoing crash.*

*'Odangidu cha (Has it broken)?' a shocked Nazar asks Joe. 'Aama,' Joe replies, stunned.*

# 'Chal, Chhotu, Bhaag!'

8 December 2021
Jaipur

Col Vijay Rawat (retired) was having a late lunch at his Banipark residence when his cellphone rang. It was his wife Sanyogita's cousin asking him to switch on the television set immediately, which he did. Vijay was horrified to see the news channels reporting that the Mi-17 taking his brother Gen. Bipin Rawat to Wellington had crashed.

He immediately called up his sister, Kiran, in the US. It was night there, but the moment she switched on the TV to watch the news from India, she said she would be coming to India. Soon after, Vijay received a call from Major General Raju Chauhan, Maj. Gen.-in-Charge, Administration (MG IC Admn.), South-Western Command, who told him that an aircraft was being sent to Jaipur to fly him to Delhi. 'I refused, saying I would prefer to drive down, as it would take the same time,' he says. Soon, the Station Commander arrived at their residence along with a staff car, which had been deputed to take them to Delhi. 'He insisted I should not take my car.'

The Rawats quickly packed a suitcase and left. As the black Maruti Ciaz sped down the Jaipur–Delhi highway, Vijay stared blindly out of the car window, his eyes clouded with tears. Desperately hoping for the best, he got lost in the memories of the brother he had looked up to all his life.

\* \* \*

January 1968
Dharamshala
6.30 a.m.

Two fair and slim Pahadi boys, crisply clad in school uniforms, badges and ties, hair neatly combed back with identical side partings, stood panting breathlessly on the parade ground, their cheeks pink from their early-morning 500-metre sprint in the cold and their backs stooping under the weight of their heavy schoolbags. They had got late having breakfast, and had to run down from their house, which was on top of the hill, to the parade ground down below, where their school bus would be waiting for them. They could see it disappearing around the bend.

Vijay, barely seven years old and studying in class two, looked tearfully at his older brother, Bipin, who was eleven years old and in class six. '*Bus miss ho gayi, Bunny* (We have missed the bus, Bunny),' he said, looking crestfallen. Bipin narrowed one eye and was looking intently at the disappearing Shaktiman truck. There was a determined look in his soft brown eyes. Taking a deep breath, he reached for his brother's hand and held it tight. '*Chal, Chhotu, bhaag. Isko mod pe pakdenge* (Let's run, Chhotu. We will catch it at the bend).'

With bags and water bottles swinging from their shoulders, the two boys raced down the nallah that dipped down steeply. They tumbled over rocks and fallen pine leaves, and zipped down the narrow mud path, which was used by the locals. Their giggles echoed in the chilly breeze. Within minutes, they had shimmied down the hillside and were at the road that had taken a full turn around the hill. When the school bus, with chattering schoolkids on board, reached the bend, the driver found the two Rawat siblings on the roadside, waving their arms in the air, and the bus screeched to a halt right in front of them.

The olive-green-uniformed soldier, holding the door open for them, a smile playing on his weather-beaten face, could not have imagined in his wildest dreams that the breathless kid climbing up the steps, dragging his brother behind him, was one day going to be India's Chief of Defence Staff. The two Rawat siblings quickly climbed up the steps mumbling 'Thank you, bhaiya' and avoided looking at their sister, Kiran, who was glaring at them fiercely from her seat.

\* \* \*

Meeting Col Vijay Rawat

Delhi Cantonment
14 June 2022

Sitting upright in an easy chair at the 5/11 Gorkha Rifles guest room in Shankar Vihar, Delhi, with fingers clasped under his chin, Col Vijay Rawat has a faraway look on his face when he shares this endearing memory of his older brother, who so suddenly disappeared from his life. There is a marked physical resemblance between the two siblings, and it would be easy for anyone to guess that they belong to the same gene pool. He has a similar smile, the same warm brown eyes, the same nose and the same strong bone structure. Beyond that, the resemblance ends. Vijay admits that though he looks a lot like his elder brother, who was four years older than him, the two were diametrically opposite in nature and temperament. While Bipin was quiet, responsible and academically inclined, Vijay was a real-world Dennis the Menace, constantly getting into trouble; and one of Bipin's growing-up responsibilities was to keep bailing his brother out, which he did uncomplainingly.

## The House on the Hill

'Early 1968, when Dad took over command of 5/11 GR at Dharamshala, we went along with him and were admitted to Sacred Heart Convent in Yol Cantonment,' Vijay says. 'Bipin was in class six, Kiran in class three and I was in class two. We had a house on top of a hill, and every morning the three of us would get ready for school and walk down to the ground that was about half a kilometre from our house, where our school bus, a big, lumbering Shaktiman, used to stop. It would take us from Dharamshala to Yol Camp. Kiran would always go to the bus stop on time, but Bipin and I would often get late having breakfast and find that the Shaktiman had already left. We would then run down the nallah and meet the road one turn ahead. Since the bus took a long, winding route, we would be able to catch it there,' he recounts.

It is, by far, one of the most charming memories of the little boy who would grow up to be India's first Chief of Defence Staff. Bipin Rawat's story, however, needs to begin from when he was born, and Vijay just relates the facts about that time, since he did not happen to be around for the next four years.

## Bunny

Bipin was born on 16 March 1958 in Dehradun. His father, then Captain Laxman Singh Rawat, was posted as an instructor at the Indian Military Academy, Dehradun, when his wife, Sushila, went into labour. The young captain rushed her to the Military Hospital, where she delivered their eldest son—a plump, healthy, fair baby boy, whom they named Bipin, affectionately called Bunny by everyone at home.

He grew up to be a model child—kind and hard-working, respectful towards his elders, protective of his younger sister, Kiran, and very fond of his youngest brother, Vijay, or the notorious Chhotu, who came into the world four years later and turned it topsy-turvy for not just the immediate family but for anyone who came in contact with him.

## Staying Up to Study with Satpal Mamaji

In November 1969, move orders came for 5/11 Gorkha Rifles, and Lt Col Rawat took his unit from Dharamshala to Ladakh. His wife and children had to shift back to Dehradun, where they took up a house in Idgah Colony. While Bipin and Vijay got admission in St Joseph Academy, Kiran started going to the Convent of Jesus and Mary. Since Sushila Rawat was staying alone with the children, her younger brother, Satpal (later Col Satpal Parmar), who was doing his graduation from DAV College Dehradun at that time, was sent by the family to stay with them. 'Bunny had a tough time with Satpal Mamaji,' Vijay remembers with a smile. 'When Mamaji's exams were going on, he would be studying till one in the night. He would make Bunny sit next to him, just so that he could have some company. Bunny, poor chap, was in seventh standard and didn't have much to study, but he was a good kid and would obediently open his books and sit up with Mamaji but would keep dozing off.'

Four years later, when Bipin was preparing for his ISC board exam (class eleven) in Shimla, he gave the same treatment to Vijay. 'Bunny was in eleventh and I was in seventh standard. He would make me stay up with as long as he kept studying. This time, I was the one who kept dropping off to sleep,' Vijay says with a smile.

## Parents in Bhutan, Days in Boarding School

In 1970, Lt Col Rawat got posted to the Indian Military Training Team (IMTRAT), Bhutan, a training mission of the Indian Army responsible for training the Royal Bhutan Army (RBA) and the Royal Bodyguard of Bhutan (RBG). Sushila Rawat joined him in Thimphu, while the children had to be put in boarding. So Bipin, Vijay and Kiran were taken out of their old schools and shifted to Cambrian Hall, which had a good boarding facility for students.

Bipin was in class eight, Kiran in class five and Vijay in class four. The boys were in the main school building, which was the old palace of Jodha Shamsher Singh, while the girls used to stay in the girls' hostel, 5 km away, and would commute by the school bus. Vijay was in the lower dormitory on the ground floor, while Bipin, being a senior, was in the higher dormitory on the first floor. With their parents away, Bipin became even more responsible towards his younger siblings.

'Bunny and I would both be dressed in the school uniform— grey trousers, white shirt and navy-blue striped tie—and being on different floors in the same building, we would run into each other almost every day. On Sunday we would get our pocket money. Since I was in the junior wing, I would be given one rupee a week, while Bunny would get two rupees a week,' Vijay says, confessing that his own pocket money would get over very soon, since he would quickly spend it on snacks and then go looking for Bipin to settle his pending dues.

'We had a nice canteen, run by an elderly balding gentleman we addressed as Mr Bob. There, we could get bun samosa for twenty paise, four nan khatais for ten paise, and even Coke, that had just arrived in India and was available for thirty paise a bottle. Needless to say, I would be having a feast all the time and would finish my pocket money. But Bunny was not a spender and always had money. I would take loans from Mr Bob after my own money got over, telling him that my brother would pay it back. Bunny would do so uncomplainingly. Sometimes, my sister would do it too. So, thanks to them, I had a great time at the boarding,' Vijay says with a happy twinkle in his eyes.

He recounts one of Bipin's birthdays, when he was sweet enough to come looking for his younger brother and offer to take him along to the canteen for a treat. 'I told him, in a very matter-of-fact tone, that I had already taken a treat from Mr Bob, and he could just go and pay for it.' Bipin nodded and did the needful. 'He never cribbed,' remembers Vijay. 'He had decided that I was his responsibility, and being my elder brother, he had to put up with all my antics, which he did with infinite patience.'

Both brothers moved in their separate friend circles but bonded over their stamp and coin collections, which they would work very hard at growing. They would coax their father to send them Bhutanese stamps, and even those from other countries, that he received in his official mail. Often, he would send them first-day covers, and when they received two identical ones, the brothers would swap the duplicate one with some other kid for a new stamp. The brothers also had a coin collection that they were passionate about. 'In fact, Bunny got a table made from that, which he kept in his house,' says Vijay.

## The Winter of 1971

When the war started, Lt Col Rawat was in Bhutan with his wife, while the children were in Cambrian Hall. In December 1971, since their school had its winter break, Bipin, Kiran and Vijay came to spend their holidays in their maternal home—14 New Road. Many of their other cousins, including Shivender, who was studying at Welham Boys' School, were also there, to spend their own winter breaks, and the children were having a wonderful time, completely unmindful of the tense situation at home with a war on at the border and Shivender's father, Lt Col Onkar Singh, in the midst of it.

## The House of Memories

Spread over an area of nearly 2.5 acres, planted with fruit trees like lychee, mango, peach and guava, 14 New Road, with nearly twenty-four rooms, was part of a cluster of three houses—Badi Kothi, Palli Kothi and the third which had had been sold and was now called Aroma Hotel. While the family would stay at Badi Kothi, the servants would be at Palli Kothi, which was 58 Lytton Road (later renamed 58 Subhash Road).

'Bunny was thirteen, I was nine. Most of the time, all of us cousins would be up on the trees, mostly the neighbours' trees, stealing their fruit,' remembers Vijay. 'They would chase us off their property shouting, "Why don't you eat the fruit of your own trees?" And we would run off shouting, "Because yours are sweeter."'

The cousins would form teams and play football or hockey using curved betel nut branches snipped off from the betel nut trees in the compound. They would invite the colony kids home and create a ruckus running around the fields, screaming and giggling. The only person who could keep the children in control was Bipin and Vijay's father, who had a cane, which both the brothers and all their cousins feared, since nearly all of them had received spankings with it. But in December 1971, he was far away in Bhutan—so the kids ran berserk, having the time of their lives.

## Roti-Eating Competitions

At 14 New Road, breakfast would be served in the dining room, Vijay recalls. It would mostly be bread and eggs, or parathas. However, the kids had their eyes on a basketful of arsa (a fried pahadi sweet made with flour and jaggery) that their nani kept in the puja room. 'We would quietly sneak past the tulsi plant outside when no grown-up was around, push our hands into the *tokri* that Nani used to keep over there and run off chewing on the arsa. Bunny would participate wholeheartedly,' remembers Vijay.

In the evening, the children would gather in the kitchen, which was on one side of the courtyard. They would sit on wooden *chaukis*, with their thalis balanced on their laps, while Bhagtu the cook, who had come from Dhanari in Uttarakhand, handed out fresh, hot rotis, straight off the griddle.

'Everything was a game for us in those days,' recollects Vijay, a smile playing on his lips. 'Often, we would have roti eating competitions, trying to beat each other at how many we could eat. When our stomachs were full, we would announce a break and go running around the courtyard a few times to build up some more appetite. We would then return and start devouring more rotis.' He laughs.

When they found the menu boring, Bipin and Vijay would ask Bhagtu to heap steaming hot rice on their plates, which they would mix with sugar and ghee and eat with their bare hands, licking the ghee dripping off their fingers. 'Those were such beautiful days,' says Vijay.

The winter was chilly. Dehradun was shivering in the freezing winds blowing in from the Himalayan range, making the water in the taps turn to sleet. The women would wrap their shawls tighter around themselves, the men would put on their woollen topis and thick khadi jackets over their sweaters, while the kids would wait for the sun to come out, so that they could climb over the garden wall and escape their homes with runny noses, which they would cunningly wipe on pullover sleeves frayed from their games of football and hockey.

They would just keep an eye out for Thakur Kishan Singh, younger brother of Bipin's Nanaji, respected politician and lawyer who had once been part of Jawaharlal Nehru's cabinet. He had retired but took care of the family home in Dehradun while Thakur Surat Singh, his older brother (Bipin's Nanaji) lived in Uttarkashi and took care of the family property there. Thakur Kishan Singh would mostly be in his study, interacting with visitors who came to him for advice and help, and the boys would avoid that area completely. His wife would spend her entire day planning meals for the extended family and shouting at the kids. Leading the brat pack was the thirteen-year-old Bunny, thin, sporty and ever-smiling in his large canvas pants and shirt, with a comfortable old sweater worn over it casually. He would be the first in for breakfast, calling out to the two Chhotus—his younger brother, Vijay, and cousin Shivender. 'Hurry up, you two. Nani is getting annoyed,' he would say, and the two of them, who had already started hero-worshipping Bunny, would quickly run down to the dining room. The boys would dig into their bread omelettes or manduve ki rotis and ghee, taking large sips from their glasses of milk. 'Fourteen New Road was a house of memories for all of us,' Vijay sighs.

## St Edward's, Shimla

In February 1972, Lt Col Rawat moved to Shimla as General Staff, Operations, GSO 1, Western Command. He decided to take his family along, not knowing at that point that his own stay there would only be two months long. In March, his wife and children joined him in Shimla, and in April, he was promoted to the rank of full Colonel and moved to Kathua, a small border town in Jammu Kashmir, as Col GS, 36 Infantry Division (now 36 Rapid). His was from the seventh batch of the Indian Military Academy which was the first batch to be given a full colonel rank. Up till then, officers used to do a long tenure as Lieutenant Colonel and then get directly promoted to the Brigadier rank.

Sushila and the children stayed on in Shimla from March 1972 to December 1973. Since Shimla lacked accommodation facilities for the army, two floors of Himland Hotel on Cart Road had been converted into lodgings and officers were given two-room suites there, where they would open their boxes and establish a home.

'When we moved to Shimla, as many as sixteen families were staying in Himland,' remembers Vijay. The Rawats were given rooms 33 and 34 on the first floor, and those became home for them for the next two years. One of the rooms had a portion that had been converted into a kitchen. The other room had study tables placed alongside the beds, so that the children could sit on their beds and place their books on the table to do their homework.

## Movies at the Ritz

The main attraction for the children in Shimla was the Ritz, a cinema on the ridge that would screen English movies. They would sneak out of the house right from under their mother's nose and make a beeline for the hall, hands jangling the painstakingly collected coins nestled in their pockets. 'My brother's pocket money had increased to six rupees by then, while I used to get four rupees per month, so naturally, I made him buy my movie tickets as well. All my own pocket money was usually spent on snacks in the school canteen or sparkling new *kanche* [marbles], that I would play against the other boys, trying to win theirs,' says Vijay, laughing at the memory.

Since the boys were staying alone with their mother, they would also help her in grocery shopping. Most evenings, the brothers would walk down to the Sabzi Mandi opposite the Ritz and come back home with their cloth *jholas* laden with vegetables and fruits for the family. In those days, no vehicles were allowed on the Mall Road in the evenings, so the walk would be leisurely and fun, even if their shoulders stooped a little under the weight of their heavy bags. 'Life was good,' says Vijay nostalgically.

## A Lifetime Bond with Sai Baba

Vijay likes to recount a life-changing incident that happened in Bipin's life and shaped his belief forever. 'Someone in Shimla hosted a programme on Shirdi Sai Baba,' he says. 'We had all heard about the miracles that Sai Baba used to perform. Bunny was so curious that he decided to attend the function with a classmate.'

The two boys went to the event after school got over. Bipin was so fascinated that he stayed back till the end. 'When he came home that evening, Bunny was completely in awe of Sai Baba. He told me he had seen stuff like *vibhooti* falling out of a picture. He returned totally converted,' remembers Vijay. 'He had become a Sai Baba devotee.'

It was to be a devotion for life. 'Prayer became a part of his daily routine thereafter, which he followed even in his busy days as COAS and CDS. He would get up early, do his pranayama and yoga, and not leave the house without praying,' Vijay says.

Vijay also remembers that Bipin had bought a silver ring from the Shirdi Sai Baba event, which he started wearing regularly from the age of fourteen; he wore the ring for the next forty-nine years, all the way till he was sixty-three. 'It was on his finger even on the day of the tragic helicopter accident,' Vijay says softly.

## Bunny Makes a Friend for Life

The boys were admitted to St Edward's, one of the oldest and most famous boys' schools in Shimla, located on Cart Road. At the red-brick-walled St Edward's, Bipin completed his class ten and eleven, and met Rohit Sarin, who would soon become his best friend. Their friendship was destined to last a lifetime. Rohit was the class topper.

'Rohit would always stand first in class,' remembers Vijay. 'Bipin would rank somewhere between fifth and tenth. The two of them were absolutely inseparable. They would sit together in class, study together after school, whether in our house, which was right next to St Edward's, or Rohit's, and even roam around Shimla together.'

Vijay remembers one evening in particular. Rohit was walking back home when he caught sight of two young boys smoking on the top of the hill, one of whom he felt was Vijay. He promptly came back and told Bipin that his younger brother had been smoking. A shocked Bipin immediately went home and told his mother. When

Vijay returned home that evening, happily humming a tune, he got the thrashing of his life from Sushila. 'I later caught up with Rohit Sarin and demanded to know how he recognized me up on the hill from so far away, and he replied that he had recognized my sweater and was duty-bound to inform Bunny.' Vijay says with a grin.

Back then, Rohit and Bipin were little boys with stars in their eyes, looking at the wonders of life in awe and making the most of it. Neither of them knew what life held in store for them. And both friends went on to do extremely well in life. Rohit became a doctor and, eventually, director of the National Institute of Tuberculosis and Respiratory Diseases; Bipin, of course, reached so high that a new rank was created in the Indian armed forces for him.

# 'Hello! My Name Is Bipin.
# Can I Sit Next to You?'

8 December 2021
National Institute of TB and Respiratory Diseases
Mehrauli, New Delhi
Around 1.30 p.m.

Dr Rohit Sarin was going through some important files in his office when, from the corner of his eye, he saw the screen of his cellphone flashing repeatedly with new WhatsApp message notifications. Curious to know what was causing the flurry of activity, he put his pen down and reached for his cell.

The notifications were from his St Edward's school group. The words 'Bipin', 'chopper crash' and 'Wellington' caught his eye, and he could feel beads of sweat appearing on his forehead. He googled for the news. Tears clouded his eyes as he prayed that his friend was alive. Images of Bipin, from his teenage years, started playing in his mind like a reel in slow motion.

\* \* \*

Class 10
St Edward's School, Shimla
April 1972

The class topper, Rohit, was sitting at his desk, deeply engrossed
in reading the underlined passages in his chemistry book, waiting
for the class to begin. Their science teacher, Brother Okeefe, had
warned them that he would be asking questions in class, and
Rohit did not want to be at the receiving end of the Bunsen
burner pipe that Brother Okeefe always carried coiled around
his hand. At the first sign of disobedience or carelessness from
a student, the pipe would curl out expertly from his hand with
a smooth flick of his palm, and before you knew it, it had hit
you on the back or the shoulder or the neck, with a hiss, leaving
behind an ugly red welt.

'Looks like we have a new admission,' someone whispered, and
Rohit looked up from his book to find a new face peering into the
classroom—the kid was short and very fair, dressed in a brand-new
school uniform. He was standing at the door, looking hesitantly
into the class, his cheeks flushed pink. He appeared so nervous that
Rohit absent-mindedly gave him a reassuring smile.

The new boy started walking towards his desk, and once he
was there, he stood shifting his weight from one foot to another.
Then, with a shy smile that reached right up to his warm brown
eyes, he said, 'Hello! My name is Bipin Rawat. Can I sit next to
you?' Rohit nodded and, shifting his books to one side, made place
for the newcomer.

* * *

## Meeting Prof. Rohit Sarin

31 August 2022
National Institute of TB and Respiratory Diseases
Mehrauli, New Delhi
1 p.m.

Professor Rohit Sarin, principal consultant and former director, NITRD, leans back in his chair in his white coat, a mask pulled over his face. His eyes look sad as he lets his mind travel back in time nearly fifty years to Shimla where, in the early '70s, he and Bipin Rawat used to study in the same class at the prestigious St Edward's School, run by the Irish Brothers. He gets lost in memories of the gentle and soft-spoken new boy in class who soon became his best friend.

He talks nostalgically about the stern Brother Okeefe, of whom all the boys were mortally afraid; the beautiful Gurmala Mehta Ma'am, their English teacher, who was just twenty and the secret crush of every boy in class. He recalls long walks that the two friends would take on Cart Road, talking about life and what it might hold in store for them, and—with a sigh—remembers those long-lost days of Archie comics and James Hadley Chase novels, of long walks on the ridge, of breathing in the crisp mountain air, of homework done together, heads bent over books and evenings spent in each other's houses, just chatting and laughing and biting into crisp hot aloo pakoras, washed down with milky chai.

'Bipin used to live in Himland Hotel, and I lived a few minutes' walk away, near the top of Cart Road, in an old, British-time cottage called Edelweiss, named after the national flower of Austria,' Dr Sarin remembers. He says they both lived so close to school that from his house they could hear the school bell; Bipin's house was even closer, and they could see their school from there. 'We would often walk down together in the morning in our uniform: grey trousers and white shirt. Sometimes, Bipin would rush out of his house, hurriedly knotting up his tie and pushing his arms into his blazer. We would also walk back together after classes got over, lost in conversation about teachers and classmates and the events of the day.'

The boys would be back by 3 p.m., having finished half of their homework in class itself on most days. The rest they would do at home, sitting together in either of their houses, after having had lunch and changed into their home clothes. 'After our work was complete, we would go on long walks along Cart Road to Chhota Shimla. Those days, it was calm and peaceful with a lot of greenery and hardly any traffic. Those were such beautiful days,' Sarin says, coming back to the present with a shake of his head.

## Meeting Bipin after Many Years

The two friends separated when Bipin cleared his National Defence Academy entrance exam and joined the NDA, while Rohit got into medical college. They had both gone their separate ways after clearing their class eleven Indian School Certificate exam. Many years later, they would meet again in Delhi, both having done brilliantly in life and established themselves in their respective careers. They easily picked up from where they had left—their friendship had withstood the test of time.

Prof. Sarin, however, admits that the Bipin he met in Delhi, who had risen like a meteor in the army, was an entirely different person from the shy kid he knew at St Edward's. While in the early stages of life, Bipin had been reticent and shy; and more of a listener, his views became very well defined later. 'He grew up to be a very different person and also a nationalist to the core,' says Sarin. The Bipin he met later in life was a leader; very confident and self-assured, ready to take the harshest decisions, knowing full well that some would go off well while others wouldn't. He could take responsibility and would not care if there were people supporting him or not. 'The one thing that had not changed was his commitment to whatever he had decided to do,' shares Sarin, recollecting how, even in their schooldays, if the two of them had decided to complete a chapter or a certain section of it, Bipin would insist that they do it without delay.

'In our schooldays, it was very easy for anyone to be friends with him, because he was quite accommodating and adjustable. He didn't have strong views or ideas, and he was very amenable to suggestion. Later, he became a man who had very clear, well-thought-out views.'

## The Shy Schoolboy Was Now a Bold, Confident Leader

The new Bipin was a man who 'could handle a situation rather than get bogged down by it', says Sarin. The little boy who had hesitated to enter a classroom had learnt to firmly control rebels in Congo, plan surgical strikes across the border, take a firm stand in support of his soldiers and walk with his head held high even in the face of criticism. 'Bipin had become a military leader. He was not a bureaucrat who would keep everyone happy,' says Sarin. So how did the quiet, hesitant kid from school metamorphose into this tough, no-nonsense General? Prof. Sarin says it was probably the military training and exposure that Bipin got.

Sarin feels that Bipin had worked on himself; he had taught himself how to overcome his weaknesses—like when he could not jump in the NDA, he came back stronger and did it. Sarin feels that Bipin had accepted the fact that he did not know a lot, and had taught himself to make an effort and learn whatever he did not know. 'He continued to read books, take lectures, to learn and adapt. I feel that was what made him what he was,' Sarin analyses.

During their time in Delhi, Bipin and Rohit would make time for each other. They would make it a point to meet at anniversaries and family functions. Though both were extremely busy with their own work commitments, they would still take out time to share confidences, just as they had done in childhood. Sarin would read reports in newspapers about the controversial decisions Bipin had taken and would sometimes ask him, '*Yaar, tu aisa kyun karta hai* (Why do you do it)?' to which the General would just smile and explain his standpoint. 'Being a doctor, I was more emotional, while his decisions would be governed by logic,' Sarin says.

When the two sat with a pre-dinner drink, Rohit would advise his childhood friend to take time out from his various commitments and responsibilities, to take care of his health, and to spend more time with his family. Madhu, sitting nearby, would just smile and say, '*Ye kabhi nahi sunte* (He never listens).'

Prof. Sarin remembers his trip to Kashmir, when Bipin was Army Commander. 'We had been chatting in the night. Later, I saw that he was reading before going to bed. I asked him, '*Kya padh rahe ho yaar* (What are you reading)?' He replied, 'Rohit, everything is useful. *Kuchh bhi padh leta hun, usko kahin na kahin toh apply kar hi lete hain. Padhne se pehle mujhe neend nahi aati. Purani aadat hai* (I read whatever I get my hands on. All knowledge can be applied somewhere. I can't sleep without reading. It's an old habit).'

When Sarin woke up the next morning, Bipin was gone. He asked Madhu about his whereabouts, and she replied that even she had no idea. Bipin had just called for his helicopter and taken off. 'Something must have come up in the night,' she said. 'He is like that. He does not tell me about work.'

Sarin shares his final memories of his friend, talking about that unfortunate day when he learnt, from the WhatsApp group of their common friends, that Bipin's helicopter had crashed. 'He had been very happy in his profession. He was satisfied that whatever he was doing, he was doing for the country. He would have done so much more but he was taken away so cruelly,' he says, his voice inflected with grief.

'What happened was so unfortunate. He was a wonderful friend. He had been a dutiful son, looking after both his parents so lovingly in their last days. And so was Madhu. She was such a wonderful person. That was God's will, so I cannot say anything, but I don't want to remember that day,' he says, wiping the tears clouding up his eyes.

# The Pretty New Class Teacher

8 December 2021
Gurgaon

Gunmala Singh was at her mother Mrs Balwant Mehta's house, engrossed in conversation with her, when her brother walked into the room and informed the ladies that Gen. Bipin Rawat's helicopter had crashed.

The two of them were aghast. It had been nearly forty years since Gunmala had first seen Bipin in Shimla. He had then been a student of class ten at St Edward's School.

\* \* \*

Summer of 1972
St Edward's School
Shimla

There was a lot of excitement in class that day. Bipin and Rohit were among the boys who had been told that they would be getting a new class teacher, who would teach them the English language as well as English literature. The boys had known the slim, small and delicately built Gunmala Mehta—daughter of Mrs Balwant Mehta—since she taught them maths in class six. When she walked in there was stunned silence in the class. It was followed by surreptitious smiles of delight as the boys nudged each other and tried to look nonchalant.

Gunmala was really pretty, unmarried and had just completed her graduation from Miranda House, Delhi. She was also twenty, so only a few years older to them. The fifteen- and sixteen-year-olds couldn't believe their luck. The rest of their faculty comprised mostly the Irish brothers, and much older and experienced teachers with grey hair, spectacles and grim expressions on their faces. So a young and attractive class teacher came like a breath of fresh air.

Though Gunmala taught them for less than two years, the boys formed with her an association for life. Decades later, when they were in their forties, they kept in touch with her. She would often invite them and their families to her farmhouse for lunch and an afternoon of rekindling old memories. Initially, though, when she first started teaching them, it was not easy to discipline them, since some of them specialized in disrupting the class.

One afternoon, when she was not around, the boys created a ruckus and caught the attention of their principal, whose office was right next to their class. He hauled them up and caned them one by one. When Gunmala got to the classroom she found them lined up outside, rubbing their sore hands, still swollen pink from the punishment.

'They tell me, even now sometimes, that I got them caned,' she says with a smile, leaning forward on the sofa in her elegantly done-up apartment in Gurgaon. 'I tell them they must have deserved it.'

She says she remembers Bipin Rawat in class ten as an industrious, hard-working and decent student. 'He was no problem at all and easily among the toppers.' Soon after the boys had written their Senior Cambridge exam in December 1973, Gunmala met her future husband, Darshan Singh, and got married, leaving the school for good. Darshan was the son of Major General K. Bharat Singh of Bharatpur. Though he loved the army, he had studied engineering and started a business instead, and went on to become an educationist and the chairman of Welham Boys' School. Since he had a close association with the army, he would often be invited to army parties and get-togethers, which was where Gunmala ran into her most famous former pupil many years later.

* * *

## 'Were You Ever in Shimla, Ma'am?'

2016
Artillery Mess
New Delhi

Gunmala Singh had been invited to dinner and was engrossed in conversation with a charming lady, who had a warm smile and was seated next to her. She had told her that her name was Madhulika. Gunmala could not help but notice Madhulika's husband—a fair, broad-shouldered and grey-haired gentleman standing nearby, looking intently in their direction. He appeared to be glaring, and Gunmala wondered if perhaps she had spoken too long with his wife; maybe they had to go somewhere, and the conversation was keeping her from that.

By the end of the evening, the gentleman walked across to her and introduced himself as Lt Gen. Bipin Rawat, Vice Chief of the Army Staff. 'Were you ever in Shimla, ma'am?' he asked her. When she replied that she had taught at St Edward's for nearly two years, he smiled and gave her a crisp salute. 'You were my teacher then,' he said, his eyes shining in pleasure. It turned out that earlier that evening, he had only been looking at her to figure out if she really was who he thought she was.

The discovery led to a lot of excitement, with those around joining in the conversation too. 'Oh! You look much older than your teacher,' someone remarked, at which Gunmala laughed and confessed to Gen. Rawat that though they were both grey-haired, she had camouflaged her age with her coloured hair. Gunmala's husband, too, walked across wanting to know what all the laughter and conversation were about, and was delighted to find that the Vice Chief was an ex-student of his wife. The two couples met many times after that, and Gen. Rawat would always come and talk to her and be extremely respectful.

Gunmala remembers one particular evening vividly. 'It was at a dinner, hosted at one of the messes, where we ran into General and Mrs Rawat again,' she says. 'He was Chief then. When they walked in he saw me there, and both of them immediately came over to chat with me.' It happened to be 16 March, which was his birthday. Later in the evening a cake was brought, which the hosts asked Mrs Rawat to cut on behalf of the birthday boy. Bipin stepped up and, much to Gunmala's embarrassment, declared with a smile, 'No, today my teacher is here, and she is going to cut my birthday cake.'

With that he walked across to her and bent over as a sign of respect. 'I didn't know how to handle it. I wasn't that much older to him, but I was quite moved by his gesture,' she remembers. So Gunmala and Bipin cut the cake while people around sang for him. And then she handed over a piece to her former student, who happened to be the Chief of Army Staff, and who, at that moment, was standing by her side and smiling widely from ear to ear.

Her eyes are sad as she leans back recollecting the terrible day when she heard about the helicopter crash that took him away. 'He was such a warm and lovely person, and so was his wife. It was a horrible way for them to go,' she says.

*Crash site*
*8 December 2021*
*Coonoor*

*The natives of Nanjappa Chatram village, about four kilometres from Coonoor, are used to seeing helicopters, since they live on the route from the Sulur air base to Wellington. They don't pay much attention to the Mi-17 flying overhead that afternoon, till they hear a loud blast. Those standing outside their houses see the chopper fall to the ground and get engulfed in a blazing inferno. Many of them drop what they are doing and rush down the hilly terrain, scampering through tea gardens to the spot where the wreckage lies burning. Angry flashes of fire are leaping into the sky, cutting through the dense mist. The blaze is so intense that no one can get close to it. Some rush back to their homes to fetch buckets of water to douse the raging fire.*

# A Chopper Crash He Survived

8 December 2021
Day of the crash
Dehradun
Late afternoon

It was a balmy winter afternoon. Retired Brigadier Shivender Singh, first cousin and childhood playmate of General Bipin Rawat, or Bunny, as he was called in the family, had just finished lunch in his airy Gajendra Vihar flat when he heard his cellphone ringing. It was a call from an officer in Wellington, who had once served with him. The Mi-17 bringing General Bipin Rawat to Wellington from the Sulur Air Force Station had crashed, he said.

Shivender was shocked. He could not believe destiny would do it twice. His mind took him back seven years in time.

\* \* \*

## The Dimapur Crash

2 February 2015
Rangapahar Military Station
Dimapur, Nagaland

Lt Col B.K. Singh, Commanding Officer of the Dimapur-based 12 (I) R&O Flight (Independent, Reconnaissance and Observation), is standing at the helipad where a stocky single-engine Cheetah helicopter awaits its VIP passenger. He spots a convoy of army vehicles heading towards him and looks down at his watch. 7.50 a.m. 'Perfectly on time, as always,' he says to himself, stepping forward to where the black Ambassador car with a fluttering flag has braked to a halt. The driver leaps out to open the door to the back seat.

Lt Gen Bipin Rawat, GOC, 3 Corps, steps out in his combat uniform. He holds a baton in hand, and his eyes are keen and bright. The top of his polished DMS boots glint in the sunlight. Though the sun is shining brightly, the general isn't wearing dark glasses. He seldom does, preferring to look into people's eyes, unhindered. His staff officer Col Anand Manwal is right behind him. The two of them are to be flown to Itanagar, where the General has a meeting with the Governor of Arunachal Pradesh. Singh shall be flying the chopper along with his co-pilot, Capt. Ksitij Gupta, a young officer on his first posting, who is already waiting in the cockpit.

Bipin steps forward briskly to shake hands with BK, who has served with him in Congo during a UN Peacekeeping Mission. Manwal has caught up too. 'Sir, it was BK's birthday yesterday. *Kal iski party thi* (He threw a party yesterday),' he tells Bipin with a mischievous smile. '*Bulaya nahi humko* (He didn't invite me),' the General jokes, placing his hand on the shoulder of a sheepish-looking B.K. Singh. 'Happy birthday, BK! God bless you.' BK has turned thirty-nine, and Manwal happens to be his National Defence Academy course mate.

Bipin walks across to the waiting chopper. At exactly 8 a.m., he takes his seat. Manwal sits on his left. BK briefs his guest, saying that the weather is clear and all routine checks have been done. The flight, he says, will take fifty-five minutes. 'Do I have your permission to fly, sir?' he asks. The General raises a thumb in the air. The two pilots strap themselves to their seats, put on their helmets and radio sets, and start the engine. Its deep, reverberating growl fills up the small helicopter. The rotors start whirring. With a roar, the Cheetah lifts into the air.

\* \* \*

Looking out of his window, Bipin has a clear view of the officers and soldiers who have come to see him off. They are holding on to their caps as the wind tries to blow them away. The draft from the powerful rotors is making their shirts billow and their trousers flap against their legs. As the helicopter rises, his eyes take in the lush greenery around the helipad and the steep drop where the helipad ends. He is a man from the hills. The beauty of the countryside never ceases to enthrall him.

His mind is already going over the points he plans to discuss with the Governor . . . But he is suddenly shaken out of his reverie. Something is not right. And then it strikes him. In the chopper, there is an eerie silence. The engine's noise appears to have stopped completely. Manwal also notices the sudden quiet. The two of them look at each other, puzzled. The pilots are bending over their instruments, and Gen. Rawat does not want to disturb them. Must be an engine snag that they will soon correct, he tells himself, looking out of the window. The helicopter is losing height and appears to be going down steadily.

The ground is rushing up very fast, and within seconds, it is in their faces. The chopper crashes into the runway with tremendous force. It strikes the concrete, throwing up a cloud of dust and scrap. Bipin covers his head with his arms in a reflex action and pushes his head into his lap. The chopper bounces up in the air from the impact and hits the ground yet again, careening forward with the ear-splitting screech of scraping metal.

Bipin can feel the seat belt tightening against him as the right side of the Cheetah suddenly dips down and the chopper turns on his side. The other side is collapsing on top of him. He can hear Manwal scream as his forehead knocks against the side of the machine. The right side has caved in completely, and Rawat closes his eyes as broken bits of metal fall on him. Around him, the stocky Cheetah shatters completely, burying its passengers in steel and debris.

* * *

### 'God Saved Us, Yaar'
8.15 a.m.
Flag Staff House, Rangapahar
Dimapur

Brig. Shivender Singh is having a relaxed cup of tea in the guest bedroom when the phone rings. He is in Dimapur on a casual visit. Shivender slips his feet into his slippers and walks across to where the army line is set up on a side table in the corridor. Bipin's young aide- de-camp (ADC) is on the line.

'Jai Hind, sir. Major Karamvir Singh this side,' he says. 'I have some bad news, sir. Commander's helicopter has had an accident.' His voice is grim.

A shocked Shivender listens as Karamvir tells him that he does not have any other details at the moment and is rushing to the helipad. Shivender asks him to send a vehicle. He says he would like to come along too. Placing the receiver back in its cradle, he returns to his room to dress. He debates whether to tell Bipin's father, Lt General Laxman Singh Rawat, former Vice Chief of the Indian Army, who is still in his bedroom, but decides against it. The frail old man has dementia. He has lost track of time and people to the extent that it is seldom that he has flashes of memory and recognizes his own son. Most of the time he just looks at him blankly, as if trying to figure out who he is. Shivender decides not to say anything to him.

He is stepping out on to the verandah when he hears the rush of vehicles. The General's convoy is entering the gate. The shining black staff car screeches to a stop in the porch, and the driver leaps out to open the door. Bipin steps out, his face grim. His uniform is shredded in places and smeared with bloodstains.

Nodding to Shivender, who is watching with concern, he says, '*Main theek hun* (I am fine).' Without uttering another word, he goes straight to his father's room. The old man is sitting up in bed, staring blankly ahead. Bipin bends down and touches his feet. His father looks at him, confused. Bipin goes out and, taking off his boots, stands in the mandir with his hands folded and his eyes tightly shut. He then steps out and goes to his own room.

A concerned Shivender follows him there, knocking on the door to ask if he can come in. '*Aaja, aaja* (Come),' Bipin calls out. Shivender enters to find that Bipin has taken off his shirt and is inspecting himself in the mirror. His vest is ripped and muddy. It is also stained with blood in places. '*Aapki shirt pe khoon laga hua hai* (Your shirt is stained with blood),' Shivender points out.

Bipin grimaces. '*Bach gaye bahut badi baat hai* (It's enough that I survived),' he says. 'God saved us, yaar. All four of us are safe.' By then, a nursing assistant has also arrived. He attends to the gashes on the General's chest and arms, applying medicine and Band-Aids where required, and gives him a tetanus shot.

As soon as the nursing assistant leaves, Bipin tells Shivender, '*Main taiyar hota hun* (I will get ready). I have asked for another helicopter.'

Shivender is taken aback. 'You have just survived a helicopter crash, Bunny,' he tells his cousin. 'Go tomorrow. Give yourself some time to relax.'

'No, I am fine,' Rawat replies shortly. '*Jana zaruri hai* (It's important to go). I have work there. People will be waiting for me. *Unhone taiyari kar ke rakhi hogi* (They must have made all the arrangements).'

Shivender reasons with him that the arrangements can easily be made again the next day. But Bipin cuts him short with, '*Sab theek hai* (Everything is all right). I have made a commitment, I shall keep it.'

Shivender knows he will not change his mind. He seldom does.

Within two hours another helicopter has been arranged. Around 10.30 a.m., Bipin walks out of the house in a fresh set of combat greens. He is looking completely relaxed and unperturbed. After a departing salute from the car, he is off.

Soon after, Shivender asks the adjutant for a vehicle and tells the driver to take him to the helipad. He is horrified to see the state of the crashed Cheetah. It has been reduced to a mass of shrunken junk. Other officers have also come to see what happened. Everyone marvels at the miraculous escape the General has had.

Many years later, sitting in his Dehradun flat, Brig. Shivender recollects that fateful February morning. 'It was a miracle that he had survived the crash. Looking at the crushed chopper, no one could have believed that its passengers were safe. But Bipin had always been a survivor.'

\* \* \*

## 'I Was the Pilot of That Chopper'

April 2021
Calcutta

Lt Col B.K. Singh, who piloted the ill-fated Cheetah on 2 December 2015, now lives in Calcutta. He has retired from the army and flies for Indigo. He fills in the gaps in the almost unbelievable survival story.

'It was a perfect morning,' he says. 'I remember the date because the day before had been my birthday, and we had had a party in our house. I was keeping close tabs on the weather, because I had to fly General Rawat to Itanagar at 8 a.m. There had been some mist in the morning, but by 7.30 a.m. it had cleared completely.'

Gen. Rawat, he recollects, had reached the airfield right on time and had been his usual jovial self. 'He had been my Brigade Commander in Congo, so we knew each other well. Soon after he boarded the chopper, I made my routine briefing and informed him that the weather was clear and the chopper had been checked for all security issues, and asked him for permission to take off. He nodded.'

The Cheetah lifted in the air as always. Down below, Singh could see the tops of the hangars where the other choppers were parked. Right ahead was a deep gorge, not forested but dense with vegetation. 'The Dimapur halidome is situated on a ledge,' Singh explains. 'It runs along the spine of the mountain, and on both sides there are deep ravines, which makes it a little risky. However, at the end of the runway there is a skirting wall that runs around the entire cantonment.'

The chopper had lifted just about seventy feet off the ground when Singh realized that its engine had failed. 'Barely six or seven seconds after take-off, our engine suddenly ceased,' he recollects. 'I was shocked. Just a couple of days back we had revised the drill and standard operating procedure for emergencies. Every morning, before take-off, the emergency drill is revised by pilots. I had been doing it all my life but never ever thought it would actually happen to me. That morning it stood us in good stead.'

So when the engine stopped, Singh's muscle memory kicked in, and he automatically started emergency procedures. 'I could see that if I did not do something fast, the chopper was going to drop into the gorge, which could be fatal. I immediately tried to turn it so that it would stay on the helipad,' he remembers. Within seconds, the chopper had crash-landed, but luckily, it happened on the runway. 'I tried to cushion the chopper's fall, but with a failed engine, there was little I could do. It hit the ground, bounced off and hit it again. The right skid gave way, making the aircraft buckle under its own weight.'

The chopper started tilting to its right, which was the side Gen. Rawat was sitting on. The rotors struck the ground and twisted, the tail rotor shattered and the fuel tank cracked, starting a deadly spill on the runway. 'The tank was full, with nearly five hundred litres of fuel. We shut down all electric gadgets, since a single spark could have blown us up,' Singh says.

By that time, the entire emergency response drill had also kicked in. The area rang out with the screams of fire engines and ambulances. Fire tenders rushed to the spot and started washing away the leaked fuel. The pilot was the first to climb out of the mangled chopper, surprising rescuers, who were fearing the worst. He was followed by the others: they emerged one by one, miraculously without any serious injury. Col Manwal had not fastened his seatbelt properly and was hit on the head, but other than that he was fine. Neither of the two pilots had even a scratch on them. Gen. Rawat had suffered the brunt of the crash, with the entire machine smashing on to his side. However, he too had just suffered some minor cuts and bruises.

The pilots were put under observation for twenty-four hours at the Military Hospital—as is mandatory—after which they were sent for an MRI (magnetic resonance imaging) to Calcutta. Singh had suffered some compression in his vertebrae but was soon back on his feet. 'The smashed Cheetah came to a stop barely five metres from the perimeter security wall. Had it toppled over, the fuel tank would have shattered and doused the engine, causing an immediate explosion.'

An unruffled Bipin had asked him for another chopper that would fly him to Itanagar. 'I explained to him that we did not have another one and also, as per the rules, I would not be able to fly him till I got a medical clearance from the hospital.' A helicopter was brought in from Dinjan, and just two hours later, it took Bipin to Itanagar.

Singh says unpleasant memories of that crash are best forgotten, but he will always remember General Rawat's complete composure after the accident. 'His uniform had been burnt in places, there were visible bloodstains but no signs of fear or anger on his face. He took me aside and said, "Just don't worry! These things happen. You did your best, don't think about it now." Gen. Rawat had this incredible ability to stay calm under all circumstances. He was a tough soldier,' recounts Singh.

# 'Hum Sab Fauj Mein Jayenge'

Brig. Shivender Singh leans back on his sitting-room sofa, nostalgia clouding his eyes. 'Bunny was an undisputed leader, even at thirteen years of age,' he says. 'He was quiet and self-effacing, but had immense clarity of thought and courage of conviction from childhood. My most striking memory of him is of the day in Dehradun when I was just nine years old, and we received news that my father had lost his life in the 1971 war.'

Shivender's father Lt Col Onkar Singh had been commanding 10 Garhwal and leading his men in battle in Chhamb, Akhnoor, when he had been hit by a bullet. His wife, Mohini, and two sons had been in 14 New Road Dehradun, Mohini's parental house, when they received the news. The 1971 war was the third one that Col Onkar was fighting in. He had also participated in the wars of 1962 and 1965, returning injured from both.

\* \* \*

14 New Road
Dehradun
December 1971
12 noon

A postman knocks on the door. He has brought a telegram. The boys see him in his old khaki sweater and pants, opening the gate and walking in, his woollen cap pulled low over his ears. 'He handed over a telegram to someone, and soon the house was filled with deep sorrow,' remembers Shivender. 'I was surprised to find my mother sobbing loudly. She held my younger brother, who was just one, in her arms. Sushila Mausi [Bipin Rawat's mother] was trying to console her. Nani was crying too. Other than that, there was stunned silence all around.'

Shivender was too young to understand the situation, but he could sense that something terrible had happened. Everyone seemed to be speaking in whispers. He was standing outside the room, scared and confused, when the thirteen-year-old Bipin walked up to him with his younger brother, Vijay, in tow. 'Bunny came to me and put his arms around me. He told me, very matter-of-factly, that my dad had lost his life in battle. "*Koi baat nahi Chotu*," he said. "Mausaji has gone down fighting. We should be proud of him."'

Seeing the alarmed looks on both his younger brothers' faces, Bipin immediately took control of the situation. '*Ab aisa karna hai, hum teeno bhi chalte hain fauj mein* (Now, the three of us should join the army). That will be our tribute to Mausaji. *Hum unka naam raushan karenge* (We will live up to his name),' he declared. When he saw the younger boys looking confused, he further said, '*Tum abhi chhote ho. Main lead karunga, tum follow karna* (You're still too young. I will you lead, you follow).'

Looking back, Brig. Shivender says those were not the empty words of an emotional teenager; Bipin actually meant what he said. He had decided his future course of action. And his inclination to lead was evident since he had decided it for his brothers as well. Three years later, Bipin cleared the National Defence Academy entrance exam and went to Khadakwasla. In the same year, Shivender and Vijay joined the Rashtriya Indian Military College (RIMC) and Sainik School, respectively. All three brothers went on to join the Indian Army. While Bipin went on to be India's first Chief of Defence Staff, Shivender retired as a brigadier and Vijay as a colonel.

## A Flashback

In 1958, General Bipin Rawat's father, then Capt. Laxman Singh Rawat, was posted at the Indian Military Academy. His wife Sushila's family were looking for a groom for her cousin Mohini. Laxman felt his friend Capt. Onkar Singh, from 10 Garhwal, who was then posted at the RIMC, was a suitable candidate and persuaded Onkar to come over to 14 New Road to meet his wife's cousin. Onkar, a Jat from Meerut, shyly agreed, and the two young army officers came over to the grand old house where Thakur Kishan Singh and the family lived. The two youngsters met and liked each other. The family approved of the handsome captain, and the two were soon married. Later, they had a son, Shivender, who adored his older cousin Bunny, and the two became friends for life just as their fathers had been.

# Bipin Joins the NDA

Towards the end of 1973, while still in Kathua, Col Rawat got promoted to the Brigadier rank and got posted to Dalhousie as Commander, 323 Infantry Brigade. He decided to move his family from Shimla and bring them with him to Dalhousie. In December 1973, after Bipin completed his ISC exam from Shimla and Vijay finished class seven, the family also shifted to Dalhousie. Bipin appeared for the National Defence Academy entrance exam, which he cleared in the first attempt. Vijay was sent to Sainik School, Lucknow, while Kiran got admitted to Sacred Heart Convent in Dalhousie.

Col Vijay Rawat recollects that while preparing for his Service Selection Board (SSB) in Dalhousie, Bipin used to go to a physical training instructor who would make him do the toughest drills, which included dives, rolls, flips, etc. During one training session, Bipin sprained his ankle so badly that he wasn't sure if he would be able to go for the SSB. But eventually, he did go for his SSB to Allahabad and went on to join the NDA's June 1974 batch.

## An Unexpected Relegation

Bipin came back home to Dalhousie, at the end of the third semester at the NDA, and told the family about his completely unexpected relegation.

'He could not do a mandatory jump into the swimming pool and had been relegated because of it,' Vijay remembers. 'I still don't know why he could not jump that day in the academy. It was really surprising. Bunny was a confident swimmer and had jumped many times before. We used to go swimming regularly in Dehradun and also Udhampur. But, for some reason, he couldn't jump on that particular day, and it led to his losing six months of seniority.'

'I remember Daddy taking it in his stride without any show of disappointment. He told Bunny, "These things happen in life. You just have to carry on regardless."'

Bipin took his father's advice well. 'There was no visible sign of low morale. We all just took it on the chin, and he went back to the academy after his winter break and cleared the jump,' says Vijay.

However, Bipin did lose six months of seniority to his NDA course mates. Many years later, in a strange quirk of fate, he superseded some of them to become Chief of Army Staff.

## Dance Nights in Udhampur

In 1976, Brig. Laxman Singh Rawat was posted as Brig. Adm. (Brigadier Administration), Northern Command, and his wife and daughter shifted to Udhampur with him. Bipin was still in the NDA, getting a monthly pocket money of Rs 40. Vijay, now in class nine at Sainik School, Lucknow, was given the option of coming back home and studying in Central School, Udhampur.

'I was getting a princely amount of seventy-five rupees a month as pocket money, which was even more than Bipin's, and so I decided that I would not shift to Udhampur, because then it would have reduced to zero,' says Vijay.

So he continued to study in Lucknow. The siblings would meet during their summer and winter breaks, and Vijay has some fond memories of those days. 'We had a lovely time in Udhampur,' he remembers. 'Bunny would come down in his term breaks, and we would do at least two or three trips to Vaishno Devi every holiday, going in the morning by bus and returning in the evening.'

'Udhampur had a good crowd,' he adds. 'There were lots of kids of our age, and we would roam around together in the holidays, play tennis and often organize social evenings where the kids would take care of the entertainment, which would mostly be songs and dance.'

Both the brothers used to enjoy dancing. Vijay remembers how they would sometimes pull each other's leg over wanting to dance with the same girl. 'There was this one friend I had. She was really good-looking, and Bunny would want to dance with her and so would I,' he says with a laugh. 'I would feel that since she was in the same class as me, I had dancing rights with her, and Bunny felt that since he was in NDA, he had the right.'

Vijay also remembers how Bipin suddenly picked up height after he went to the academy. 'Before Bunny left for NDA, he was hardly five feet three inches. I used to be taller than him. When he came back from NDA, he had shot up to five eight.'

The Udhampur Club had a nice swimming pool, where the brothers would go for regular swims and try to beat each other at the number of lengths they could do. Their strong, sunburnt arms would cut the water in measured strokes as they raced. Whoever reached the end of the pool first would turn around and, shaking water out of his eyes, would look out for the other.

## The Notorious Chhotu

While Bipin was always the responsible and sensible older son, he always stood by his notorious younger brother. Vijay confesses that he was in and out of trouble all the time. 'I had so many scars on my body that I used to be called Rana Sangha in childhood,' he states proudly. In Dehradun, he had been badly bitten by a neighbour's ferocious Alsatian, and Bipin and Satpal mamaji would take him for his fourteen injections. As soon as that wound healed, he fell upon barbed wire while climbing to the roof of his house and received a deep gash on his leg, all the way to the bone. Once again, he had to be given medical help. At Wellington, he was swinging on the iron gate outside his house, when the gate fell on him, breaking his leg. In Shimla, he was caught smoking by Bipin's classmate who told Bipin and Bipin informed his mother, which led to Vijay getting a good telling off when he reached home.

In Udhampur, he was doing a backflip into the pool one day when he hit his head against the cemented side, splitting his head open and had to be rushed to the military hospital. And much later, when he was commanding his unit, he even got bitten by a viper that happened to be coiled around a curtain that he had tried to draw. 'The snake fell on my leg and bit me, but its fangs could not inject the venom, and I was back home the next day after spending a night at the Military Hospital's intensive care unit,' he recalls. The unfortunate snake was hunted down and killed, but the next day Vijay started getting calls from people who said to him, 'We heard you were bitten by a snake and the snake died!'

In spite of their different temperaments, both brothers remained really close to each other in their growing-up years.

# Bloody-Nosed in the IMA
## Boxing Ring

8 December 2021
Vivek Vihar
Sector 82, Noida

Major General Shashi Bhushan Asthana, SM, VSM (retired), took
one last look inside his suitcase and snapped it shut. In half an hour
he planned to leave for the airport, from where he had a flight to
Rajkot. His cell was ringing. Reaching into his pocket, he drew it
out. The call was from Doordarshan. The person calling him wanted
to know if he had heard the tragic news about Gen. Bipin Rawat's
helicopter crash. He wanted some quotes from Gen. Asthana.

A stunned Gen. Asthana switched on the television. The story
was raging across all the news channels. As he picked up his suitcase
to leave, his mind was still numb with shock. 'The rescue team shall
find him alive,' he told himself. He knew Bipin Rawat was not a
man who gave up easily. He had always fought till the last.

\* \* \*

Early 1978
Training area, Tons Valley
Indian Military Academy
Dehradun

The boxing ring is surrounded by second-termers—Gentleman Cadets who look almost identical, with their crewcut hair, PT shorts and excited faces, their skin sunburnt and peeling from long hours in the outdoors, their muscles stretched taut from rigorous physical activity. 'Come on, Rawat! Give up now!' someone is shouting.

Bipin doesn't look up. He is bleeding from the nose but circling his opponent like a prowling tiger. Lean, muscular, with almost zero fat from his gruelling schedule, he has thrown and blocked as many punches as he could, but now each jab is getting harder. His arms feel like lead. His face is swollen. He is fast running out of energy. His opponent is much stronger than him. Not only is he bigger, but he also moves really fast for his size, which has surprised Bipin. The GCs and Directing Staff watching the match can see who the better boxer is. For every punch Bipin throws, he is getting two back. The larger boxer suddenly steps forward and, pivoting on his left foot, bends his arm 90 degrees, landing a bone-splintering right hook on Bipin's left jaw. Bipin finds himself on the floor. He looks up to find the referee looking down at him in concern. 'Do you want to continue?' he asks. Bipin can taste blood in his mouth. He moves his tongue to check if any teeth have been dislodged, but they appear intact. 'Do you want to opt out?' the referee asks again. Wiping the blood off his face, Bipin pulls himself up back to his feet and replies, 'No, sir.'

The round restarts. His opponent steps forward and moves purposefully in his direction. Spitting blood on the floor, Bipin rocks on his feet and darts a quick look at the ringside. His friends from the Zojila company are looking up at him, concern writ large on their faces, their hope fading. If he loses, they shall go back disappointed. 'Rawat, it's okay. Well played. *Ab wapas aaja* (Now return),' someone is saying. By the time Bipin notices his opponent's muscular arm coming at him and tries to duck, it is too late. The punch connects, ripping the flesh on his cheek. The rival company cadets roar in anticipated victory.

Bipin can feel his head reeling. His mind is now numb to pain. Trying desperately to keep his balance, he bites down on his mouth guard, swings his right arm back and, with all the strength remaining in his battered body, throws an upper cut at his adversary. He is surprised to find that it has connected. And suddenly, his opponent is lying flat on the floor. As he stumbles forward, Bipin hears the victorious yelling and screaming of his friends. He cannot believe his eyes. He has won.

## Passing Out with the Sword of Honour

Maj. Gen. S.B. Asthana, Chief Instructor, United Services Institution of India, sits upright in his office chair, looking dapper in his Gorkha hat and waistcoat, as he time-travels back to the Dehradun of 1978, when he and Bipin Rawat used to be course mates and company types from the Zojila company at the Indian Military Academy.

'I was twenty, and Bipin must have been a year younger,' he says. 'I remember that boxing bout very clearly. I was not on the boxing team that day, but I was standing by the ring. In fact, our entire company had lined up to watch the fight. It was obvious that the other guy was not just bigger in size but also a better boxer technique-wise. Nobody expected Rawat to win, but he just refused to give up. He kept taking a beating, but he would get up each time he fell, and the bout would go on. And eventually he won, surprising everybody.'

Though he was just a second-termer, Bipin became the star of the IMA after that match. The quiet, unassuming cadet, who generally kept a low profile, had been recognized as a gritty fighter who had refused to give up against all odds. 'The DS were talking about him, the cadets started looking up to him, and it gave him instant recognition. He had displayed exemplary officer-like qualities,' says Gen. Asthana.

## 'He Was a Spotlessly Clean Man'

Bipin Rawat joined the 63 Regular Course at the Indian Military Academy in January 1978. Since he had come from the NDA, he joined in the second term, but because he had been relegated, his NDA course mates were now one course senior to him. He was given certain privileges of a third-termer. For instance, he did not have to address third-termers as 'Sir', and they would not rag him like they ragged the others.

Gen. Asthana remembers Bipin as a simple and unassuming guy. 'He was a course senior to us, but he never made that obvious,' he says. 'He would do everything that the rest of us had to do. Sometimes we would get late for class, and the DS would tell us to get off our bicycles and carry them on our shoulders. He would do it with the rest of us, uncomplainingly. And even though his father was a serving Brigadier, he never made that obvious. We had heard that even in his own house, he would do his own work and pick up his own luggage, in spite of the fact that his father had *sahayaks* (attendants). That was obviously how he had been groomed. He was humble and grounded.'

So Bipin Rawat marched down the roads of the IMA in his beige dungarees, with his course mates by his side, a *pithu* on his back and his feet bound in heavy, black DMS boots. He would sometimes be seen dragging along his black bicycle, or carrying it over his head. He was quiet and sincere, gritty and determined. 'He was easily among the better guys,' says Gen. Asthana. 'And then he got the Sword of Honour too.'

\* \* \*

Kritika's wedding
5 March 2017
Army House
4 Rajaji Marg

Maj. General Asthana parks his car and walks down to Army House, where shamianas are stretched across the lawns and the guests have already started collecting. The house is glittering with strings of lights, and he can see elegantly attired ladies and men in formal wear, smiling and moving around the place. Since it is a largely an armed-forces crowd, many of them know each other. Gen. Asthana spots Brigadier Sohi, Military Attaché to the Chief, whom he knows from earlier. He steps across to shake hands.

'Where is Rawat?' he asks Brig. Sohi.

'Sir, *mujhe bhi dhundna padega* (I have to look for him),' he smilingly replies. 'Today, I am also an invitee.'

\* \* \*

'Bipin had taken over as Chief of Army Staff in January. His daughter Kritika got married in March. There was so much the army could have done, but he just refused to take any favours. The arrangements were as simple and affordable as they would have been at a Colonel's daughter's wedding,' says Gen. Asthana. 'Bipin had invited his entire staff as guests, and all arrangements were being looked after by his family, who could be identified by the identical *safas* that all the men were wearing. A civil caterer had been hired to put up tents and make all arrangements. The guests had been accommodated in a modest hotel that he had paid for. Bipin Rawat was standing there in a bright-yellow turban, smiling, personally looking after each invitee.'

Gen. Asthana says the marriage was a window into the kind of person Bipin was and into his beliefs. 'He was a spotlessly clean man,' he says. 'Nobody could question him on his personal integrity and honesty. It was his daughter's wedding. As Chief, he could have utilized so many Army resources. He didn't even have to say it. People would have come forward on their own. But he didn't do anything of that kind. He was absolutely honest. He was also conscious that he should not be doing anything that could lead people to point a finger at him, saying he had misused his position.'

## 'Once He Had Decided Something, He Was Unwilling to Change His Mind'

Gen. Bipin Rawat took many bold decisions during his tenure, and not all of these were universally liked. He caused a lot of heartburn in the 1.1 million-strong force by his moves to do away with the sahayak concept, disallowing golf in active forward areas of Jammu and Kashmir and Nagaland, and taking strong measures to get officers and men off social media, which had been previously used to honey-trap men in uniform.

Just a few months before he was to retire as COAS, Gen. Rawat ordered an analysis to understand why the Indian Army's pension bill was rising, accompanied by a rise in disability pension, particularly in non-combat situations. The analysis, done by Army Headquarters, revealed that a large number of officers had claimed disabilities for non-physical injuries, such as hypertension, diabetes, hearing loss and other ailments. So it was a clause that was being misused by many, since the army gives a very generous non-taxable disability pension even for non-battle casualties, which ranges from 30 per cent to 15 per cent of last basic pay drawn, depending on the level of disability. Gen. Rawat had briefed Union Defence Minister Rajnath Singh, and Finance Minister Nirmala Sitharaman had given a statement in Parliament on not allowing tax exemption on disability pension. Further reforms were awaited. The move caused a lot of anger within the army, since it would also affect the genuinely disabled.

'I had questioned him on why he was trying to cut everything from the army. "*Tu defence civilians ko kuchh kyun nahi kehta* (Why don't you say something to the defence civilians)?" I had asked him, to which he had replied, "*Wo toh mere haath mein nahi hai. Main kya karun* (That's not in my hands. What can I do)?" If he was convinced about something, he would not listen to anyone. That was Rawat's personality. His logic was that he wanted to stop people who were creating a fake disability and drawing pension for it. I told him he should sort out those guys and not punish everyone, including those who genuinely deserved disability pension and concessions. But he had that typical Gorkha "mancha" mindset; once he had decided something, he was unwilling to change his mind,' Gen. Asthana says.

Many officers like Gen. Asthana wrote vociferously against the idea in newspapers and spoke about it on television. The collective pressure worked, and so far the government has not implemented what Gen. Rawat had proposed.

\* \* \*

Later, when Gen. Rawat became Chief of Defence Staff, initiatives proposed by his Department of Military Affairs aimed at increasing the retirement age of officers and jawans, and a reduction in pensions of personnel taking premature retirement. These decisions were also extremely unpopular.

In January 2020, soon after he was appointed CDS, Gen. Rawat started working on what was to be India's biggest-ever military reform: theatre command. He wanted to streamline coordination between the army, navy and air force, and have synchronized operations in future wars, as happens in the US and China. Instead of having them as separate forces, he wanted to reorganize them into theatre commands that would draw commanders from all three services.

Gen. Rawat envisioned that the existing seventeen single-service commands would then be reduced to five, and the forces would be able to function with better integration and harmony. The suggestion did not find favour with the air force. 'The air force had a valid reason to worry,' explains Gen. Asthana. 'They are short of critical aircraft and other air assets. Most aircraft are multirole aircraft. If you give away their already meagre resources to theatres, how would they look after air defence?'

Gen. Asthana says he did try to reason with Gen. Rawat that before bringing about a theatre command, he needed to improve the resources of the air force, but Gen. Rawat was totally convinced about his decision. To initiate the plan, a joint three-services course at the Brigadier level was started at the United Service Institution of India, which is still going on.

## 'He Believed His Decisions Were for the Greater Common Good'

Gen. Asthana says Bipin was completely aware of the immense criticism some of his proposals were facing within the forces, but since he believed they were for the greater common good, he did not care. 'The army expects the Army Chief to look after the army, but Rawat's approach was a whole-nation approach, which would upset people in uniform. For instance, he opened the cantonment roads to civilians, because he felt the citizens of the country should not be inconvenienced because of the army. But the fact is that army units are often training inside cantonments. They have weapons, armouries, exercises going on, and granting access to just anyone means a Pakistani agent could make a video or take photographs and send it across. Similarly, he agreed to give away defence land to the government. How do we know that the army will not require additional land for training and exercises, and that it will be put to better use by the politicians? The idea of land monetization needed careful scrutiny, as the funds so generated go to the Consortium Fund of India and not directly to the military,' feels Gen. Asthana. He adds that he conveyed these misgivings to Gen. Rawat, who would just brush them off.

Gen. Asthana believes that Bipin Rawat did not have any political aspirations or personal motives for these decisions. 'Rawat was a true nationalist and was convinced that whatever he was doing was for the good of the country,' he says. 'When he was convinced about something, he had the mental strength, which his critics used to call arrogance, to not get swayed by other people's opinions or criticism.'

## 'PM Modi Liked Him a Lot'

Whatever his vision was, the fact remains that Gen. Bipin Rawat was very popular with the government. 'Prime Minister Narendra Modi liked him a lot, and he had reasonable freedom of action with the PM, which not very many can claim,' states Gen. Asthana. He feels this was because Gen. Rawat had learnt how to handle bureaucrats and politicians, thanks to his long work experience in Army Headquarters.

'"Can I fight with the government and get anything for the services?" he would often ask, stating how the government was supreme in a democracy. "When I can't fight with the government, I might as well get the best out of them," was his logic for going along with what the government said. He would be finding ways to do things. "Whenever I am working with politicians or bureaucrats, the moment I find a block, I try to find an alternative route around it instead of banging my head against the wall," he would often say. . . As a person who knew him well, I would say that he certainly did not want to become a politician, but he also certainly did not want to cross politicians and make his functioning difficult. He was a practical man, and he was adopting a practical approach while dealing with politicians, so that they did not block his moves,' Gen. Asthana explains.

## 'He Knew How to Handle Politicians'

In 2002, then Col Asthana was posted at Army Headquarters, serving in the Operational Logistics department. Then Col Bipin Rawat was also at Army Headquarters, serving as Colonel, Military Secretary Branch 9. His job profile included coordinating Military Secretary Branch matters. This was his second tenure there. About a decade back, he had served in the Military Operations department as a Major.

Gen. Asthana feels that these interactions taught him how to handle bureaucrats and politicians. He says, 'Even in his days as a Colonel he would say, "*Government se kaam karaane ke liye* (To work with the government) you need to know what they need, then you decide *kaam kaise karaana hai* (how to make them work)." He had learnt to sideline his ego. He would say, "*Finally toh undersecretary sign karega, tabhi government order banega* (Once the undersecretary signs, only then would the government order be ready), so I should not be rigid and be willing to explain, even if he questions me ten times.'"

## 'He, Too, Faced Failure'

Gen. Asthana also points out how Gen. Rawat had to face his fair share of disappointments in his career. 'It wasn't as if he was handed everything on a platter or that he got success each time. He, too, had to face failure, but Rawat handled it very well.'

As an example, he remembers the time when Gen. Rawat attempted to go for a UN assignment. Interviews for these are held at Army HQ, and officers are selected on merit. 'When Rawat was Col MS9, he was under Lt Gen. Richard Khare, who was MS. Both of them were from the Gorkhas, and one would have thought it would be easy for Rawat to get selected for a UN tenure, since MS conducts interviews for the same, but that was not so. He went for two or three interviews over a period of three years—from 2002 to 2005—but got rejected every time, because there would be one officer better than him who would get selected. Eventually, he did not get a UN assignment as a Colonel, but he did not let that deter or disappoint him. He continued to work hard. He did very well in MS Branch, and then he moved on. Eventually, as a Brigadier, he did go on a UN mission to the Democratic Republic of the Congo, where he commanded the United Nations Organization Stabilization Mission, MONUSCO, and did an excellent job.'

Gen. Asthana also points out how Gen. Rawat never picked easy tenures. Gen. Rawat was serving at Army HQ when he got his promotion as a Brigadier. Since he was in MS Branch, he could have chosen the brigade he wanted to command, but he picked Rashtriya Rifles, which is an unlikely choice with most people, and he picked Sopore, which was a hard and active field. Gen. Asthana points out that most hardcore soldiers want to command in field areas, because there are fewer non-professional pressures there. You are analysed and judged for professional issues. 'Eventually, it was good move for his career too,' he says.

Bipin Rawat was an ambitious man. 'But ambition is not a bad thing,' says Gen. Asthana. 'Most officers who are doing well are ambitious. For Rawat, I will vouch for the fact that he never compromised on anything for that ambition.'

*Crash site*
*8 December 2021*
*Around 12.25 p.m.*

*Twenty-four-year-old Sangeeta, of Nanjappa Chatram village, is one of the first persons to reach the burning chopper. She joins the others in trying to put out the raging fire by flinging buckets and pots of water on it. There are more blasts as the flames leap higher into the air. Sangeeta feels she hears someone crying out for help, but every noise gets drowned in the crackle of flames. So much heat has been generated that the villagers cannot get close to the burning chopper, even though they try.*

# Ayo Gorkhali!

8 December 2021
Sansad TV Studio
New Delhi

Lt Gen. Rakesh Sharma, former Adjutant General of the Indian Army and now a renowned defence analyst, was walking out of the Sansad TV studio, having just completed an intense interview moderated by Dr Maroof Raza. Drawing his cellphone out of his pocket, he switched it back on and was looking at it absent-mindedly when his heart suddenly missed a beat.

'Air Force helicopter taking Gen Bipin Rawat and wife Madhulika to Wellington crashes,' said a message flashing on the screen. Gen. Sharma took a moment to collect his thoughts, drove down to his house in Greater Noida and, picking up his wife, headed straight for the Chief of Defence Staff residence at Kamraj Road.

Hands on the steering wheel of his car, he drove in silence as his mind travelled back to the year 1979, when he first saw Bipin as a young and handsome Second Lieutenant.

\* \* \*

Winter of 1979
Amritsar Railway Station

The sun was shining brightly. A young Gorkhali officer in combat
uniform and DMS boots stood at the platform stomping his feet
impatiently. He was Second Lieutenant Umed Singh Thapa of 5/11
Gorkha Rifles. He had come to receive 2Lt Bipin Rawat, the new
twenty-one-year-old officer joining their unit and had removed his
epaulettes, showing his rank, for a reason. Since Bipin was the son
of Brigadier Laxman Singh Rawat, former Commanding Officer
of 5/11 GR, and had also been awarded the Sword of Honour for
topping his course at the Indian Military Academy, the unit officers
had decided that he needed to be cured of any airs he might have
developed and had to be brought back to mother earth.

A mischievous plan had been hatched to rag Bipin, and it was
now being put into action. It also added some excitement to the
lives of the officers and men, who were a little bored with their
staid regimental tenure at Khasa, a small army cantonment near
the Wagah border, about 14 km from Amritsar. Thapa had driven
down to the railway station in a jeep, bringing along a one-tonne
(truck) for Bipin Rawat's luggage. Being a Gorkhali, he had been
chosen to pose as Bipin's sahayak.

With narrow, twinkling eyes and a guileless smile, Thapa
was tailormade for the role. All he had to do was remove his
rank insignia. He had been tasked to receive Bipin and steal his
identity card. A delighted Thapa had rubbed his hands in glee and
immediately agreed. The then Commanding Officer of 5/11, Lt
Col (later Brigadier) Ravi Devasar, was out of the unit location for
some official work that day and completely unaware of the mischief
brewing behind his back.

There was the wail of a horn, and Thapa looked up to find a
train thundering down the tracks. The noisy steam engine rushed
past him, pulling along its cavalcade of bogies. As the train whined
to a stop, Thapa hastily put on his jungle cap and, reminding the

four Gorkha troops with him to not address him as 'Sahab' in front of Bipin, started walking along the platform to look for his guest.

'*Pahilo kaksako dibba*,' he called out, pointing towards the first class carriage from where a smartly uniformed and slim Pahadi officer was stepping down—beads of perspiration on his face, cheeks red from the effort of pulling down his shining black steel box, which now rested on the platform. Stencilled on the side of the box, in bold white font, was '2Lt Bipin Rawat, Indian Military Academy, Dehradun to Amritsar'. It left no doubts about the identity of the officer who, at that moment, was busy dragging down a heavy khaki canvas bedroll with thick leather straps.

Thapa broke into a quick sprint and was there by Bipin's side in a flash. '*Ram Ram, hajur*!' he bellowed, clicking his heels together and bringing his arms smartly to attention. '*Ma timro sahayak hun* (I am your sahayak).'

Bipin saluted him back. '*Tapaiko I card deno parcha. Adjutant Sahab le mangarnu bhaeko cha* (You will need to give me your identity card. Adjutant Sahab has asked for it),' Thapa informed Bipin in Nepali, blinking innocently. By then, the other soldiers had picked up the luggage waiting on the platform. Bipin reached into his pocket and handed over his identity card to Thapa. Thapa led him to the jeep waiting outside and, instructing the driver to drive the 'new saab' to the unit location, assured Bipin that he would follow in the one-tonne along with the luggage.

In twenty minutes, the jeep had driven into the unit location, where the sentry on duty quickly gave a call to the main office, announcing the new sahab's arrival. 2Lt (later Lt Gen.) Rakesh Sharma, also a participant in the mischievous plan, scampered across the corridor to ensconce himself firmly in the unit adjutant's chair just before Bipin marched in. He greeted Sharma with a crisp salute. '2Lt Bipin Rawat reporting, sir!' he said.

'Good morning, Rawat!' Sharma replied, looking up from the papers he had pretended to be busy signing. 'Welcome to the unit! Let me see your identity card, please.'

A puzzled Bipin replied that he had already handed over his ID card to his sahayak, who, he was told, would be delivering it to the adjutant.

'No one has given it to me,' Sharma exclaimed, looking a little miffed. 'Who is your sahayak?' When Bipin looked unsure, Sharma summoned the boys who had gone to pick him up from the railway station. 'Which of them is your sahayak?' he asked. A bewildered Bipin could not identify the man, since all the fair and slim Gorkha boys looked similar to him. Also, Thapa had not made an appearance at all in the identification parade.

A seemingly exasperated Rakesh Sharma sat tapping his fingers on the table impatiently as Bipin confessed he could not identify the man. 'Well! You seem to have lost your ID card. That is very careless of you. I am taking this very seriously,' Sharma told Bipin coldly, hiding a smile. 'I will have to march you up to the Commanding Officer.'

A nervous Bipin was taken to the CO's office, where, in the absence of Col Devasar, Senior Captain Madan Gopal was comfortably seated on the CO's chair with a stern expression on his face and a Lt Colonel's brand-new epaulettes (borrowed that same morning from the unit Baniya) sparkling from his shoulders. 'You are a Sword of Honour from the academy, right?' he asked after the introduction had been made, nodding grimly at the mention of the missing ID card.

When Bipin answered that he had topped his course, Gopal told him that Bipin would have to complete the Battle Physical Efficiency Test (a two-mile run) to prove how fit he was. 'Since you are the best in your course, we expect you to finish in the excellent category,' Gopal said.

Bipin was driven down to the highway in his uniform, handed over a 4 kg self-loading rifle (SLR) and told to run towards the Wagah border, all the way to the turning point, and to return only after collecting a ticket from the *kanchas* (boys) manning it. The two-mile stretch was the unit's regular cross-country route and pre-marked, he was told. Though tired and frustrated, and with an angry winter sun bearing down hotly upon his head, Bipin made no excuses and immediately set off on a quick sprint, returning with the required ticket.

He was surprised to find that he had not been able to meet the 'Excellent' finish time of fourteen minutes and forty-five seconds. The run had taken him longer than that. He did not know that the crafty ragging team had got the ticket collection post shifted by 400 yards so he had to run an extra distance, which increased his timing.

He was again marched up to the CO, who glared at him darkly this time. 'I must say that I am disappointed in you, Rawat. It is shocking to find that a Sword of Honour could not make it to the Excellent category,' Madan Gopal growled at the shamefaced Bipin. 'Just because your father is a Brigadier and an ex-CO doesn't mean you will now take it easy and can sleepwalk through your regimental tenure. Pull up your socks!'

The adjutant marched a morose Bipin out of the CO's office and told him to report for physical examination to the Military Inspection (MI) Room, where yet another trickster, 2Lt Utpal Roy, sat with a borrowed Army Medical Corps badge on his uniform and a stethoscope hanging casually around his neck. He was raring to show off his own acting skills.

'Who are you? I've never seen you before,' he snapped, playing the absent-minded unit doctor, the moment Bipin walked in.

'I am 2Lt Bipin Rawat, sir. I have just been posted in,' Bipin replied.

'You don't look happy, my boy. What's the problem?' Roy asked, shining a flashlight into Bipin's eyes while pretending to do an ophthalmic examination.

'No, sir, I am not happy,' Bipin replied.

'Hmmm!' Roy mumbled, asking him to open his mouth wide and stick out his tongue. After peering down Bipin's throat for what seemed like an eternity, Roy took the spatula off his patient's tongue and asked him to close him mouth. 'And why are you not happy, my dear?' he asked, raising his eyebrows.

His dam of tolerance broken, Bipin gave the overtly sympathetic Roy a blow-by-blow account of what had transpired with him. Being a second-generation officer, familiar with the ways of the army, he was smart enough to understand that he was being ragged but had completely run out of patience. 'Is this how a young officer should be treated, sir?' he asked, looking harassed.

Roy clicked his tongue in disapproval. 'Shameful indeed! These Gorkhas, I tell you! Why did you join this unit at all, my boy? You shouldn't have,' he muttered sympathetically.

The gullible Bipin immediately opened up his heart to the kind doctor, the only nice person he had met that day. 'I wanted to join Mechanized Infantry, sir,' he said. 'And being the course topper, I would have got it too. But Uncle Heera [Lt General R.D. Heera, then Colonel of the regiment] insisted that I should opt for 5/11 GR, since my father had commanded it,' he replied honestly.

Roy nodded in sympathy and, after pretending to check Bipin's chest with the stethoscope he had till then forgotten to use, told him that all was well, the medical examination was over, and he could go to his room.

At lunch that afternoon, CO Col Devasar returned to the unit and a dining-in was hosted for the new joiner. When Bipin walked into the mess, the other officers were already there, this time in their proper uniforms, wearing their right ranks. He was greeted with warm handshakes. As he stood in the gathering with a glass of chilled beer in his hand, the culprits of the morning misadventure walked up to him one by one, introducing themselves, mischievous smiles lighting up their young faces.

Bipin was surprised to find Thapa, his missing sahayak, turning up with shining single stars upon his shoulders. 2Lt Rakesh Sharma took Bipin's ID card out of his pocket and handed it over with a deadpan look on his face. They were both from Dehradun, both Pisceans with just a year's difference in their ages and their birthdays falling a day apart (Bipin's birthday was on 16 March and Rakesh's on 15 March).

'Welcome to 5/11 GR, Bipin. Don't lose your ID card again,' Sharma said and finally broke into the laughter he had been controlling since morning.

'Thank you, sir,' Bipin replied with a smile spreading slowly across his face. It was to be the beginning of a lifelong friendship between the two of them.

# The Bachelor with Gentle Brown Eyes

Leaning back on the sofa in his elegant Greater Noida apartment, Lt Gen (retd) Rakesh Sharma, PVSM, UYSM, AVSM, VSM, former Adjutant General of the Indian Army, has an affectionate smile on his face as he remembers his friend Bipin, the twenty-one-year-old Pahadi boy with gentle brown eyes and neat crewcut hair who had marched into the 5/11 GR adjutant's office forty-three years back and had saluted him smartly.

'I was just a year older than him,' he says. 'We had struck up a friendship almost instantly.' The two went on to serve together, off and on, in the unit, initially as young Second Lieutenants and then as Commanding Officer and Second-in-Command (2IC) when Rakesh took over the unit and Bipin became his 2IC. Much later, the two served together in Delhi, when Lt Gen. Rakesh Sharma was serving as Adjutant General of the Indian Army and Lt Gen. Bipin Rawat was appointed Vice Chief of Army Staff and later Chief of Army Staff. Rakesh had also done a tenure as ADC with Bipin's father, Lt Gen. Laxman Singh Rawat. He was present at Bipin's as well his sister Kiran's weddings, and was by his friend's side when he lost both his parents.

As 2IC in Binnaguri, with Rakesh as the Commanding Officer, Bipin would often come to the Sharmas' house for dinner and demand to know from Payal Sharma: 'Ma'am, *ye batao dessert mein kya bana hai* (Tell me what's for dessert)?' She would always have an extra serving ready in the fridge that the two friends would devour after the last guest had left, sitting at the dining table with spoons in their hands, cracking jokes and eating straight from the dessert bowl.

'I would see the two of them in deep discussion, sometimes agreeing and often disagreeing with each other, lost in fierce arguments. But at the end of it they would come to the dining table and end the evening with large helpings of dessert. They both had a sweet tooth,' Payal recollects with a gentle smile.

Gen. Sharma's memories go back much further. 'That day in Khasa, when we ragged Bipin, he did see through our charade. He was way smarter than us and, being the son of an ex-CO, he knew our names from before, but he just played along,' he says. 'Later he told me, "*Mujhe pata tha aap kaun hai* (I knew who you were)." And we both had a good laugh. The gag just brought us closer.'

## Tripling on a Black Yezdi

Halfway through its Punjab posting, 5/11 GR moved from the ramshackle Khasa distillery location to Govindgarh Fort near the Amritsar railway station. While earlier, the young officers used to share rundown, crumbling rooms, they now had their own smartly turned out bachelor pads.

2Lt Roy had bought a stylish black Yezdi motorcycle, and often, Roy, Rakesh and Bipin would go tripling on it, jostling each other for space. 'We would scout the city restaurants for interesting meals whenever we needed a break from mess food,' Gen. Sharma remembers.

While the three of them would mostly ride on the same bike, if another bachelor decided to come along, they would borrow a scooter from someone or take the unit one-tonne and go rocking over Amritsar's roads in *fauji* style. The unit one-tonne had been converted into a fairly comfortable bus, with seats placed along both sides. The youngsters would pile in and happily be driven down to the city, jumping out of the back when the truck parked outside the restaurant they wanted to eat at. Meal over, they would troop back to the one-tonne and, climbing up one after another, ask the driver to head back to the cantonment.

Soon, their CO, Lt Col Ravi Devasar, got posted out of the unit, and Lt Col S.K. Chakravarty took over as the new Commanding Officer. He appointed Bipin as his Intelligence Officer (IO), while Rakesh sat on the adjutant's chair. 'Bipin was bright and forthcoming from the beginning,' remembers Gen. Sharma. 'He was well-read and well-informed, and could chat and converse on any subject, never hesitating to speak his mind.'

Young officers normally avoid speaking out in the presence of seniors, but Bipin had no reservations about expressing his opinion. '5/11 had a friendly crowd of senior officers who encouraged youngsters to participate in discussions. That was the culture in our unit,' Gen. Sharma explains. 'We didn't believe in the maxim that young officers should be seen and not heard. They would be asked their opinions during discussions, and they would be heard.'

This was something that would stay with Bipin all his life. He always had a reputation for plain-speaking, even as he rose through the ranks and was expected to be more diplomatic. He would express his opinion clearly and bluntly, whether he was addressing army gatherings or the media, or even interacting with his own family members, who always preferred to approach his wife rather than him when it came to asking for any kind of favours. Madhulika would be sweet and sympathetic, and would convey the requirements to Bipin seeing the right time and mood. Sometimes he would get convinced and sometimes he wouldn't. He never learnt the art of diplomacy and would often be criticized for being brash when he was only being forthright, without bothering about the fact that he might be judged for it.

'Yes, he spoke his mind all his life, starting from when he was just a Second Lieutenant,' agrees Gen. Sharma. 'And why not? He was intelligent, sharp, confident. He had studied at the best schools in the country. What's more! He was a Sword of Honour, the top man in his course.' He emphasizes that even though Bipin had come to the unit with a Sword of Honour tag, he still had to validate his worth in front of the troops.

## Earning the Respect of Gorkha Troops

The Gorkhas had the reputation of being gutsy warriors, and Bipin would have to prove the same to them before earning their respect. Which he did very soon. The opportunity came when the unit was sent on a canal-crossing drill, a common infantry war preparedness exercise in the western sector (Punjab and Rajasthan), where the ditch-cum-bund (DCB) system of warfare is propagated. Soldiers have to cross a water body that cannot be surmounted by a tank and then attack the enemy, who is expected to be on a raised piece of land behind it.

The Gorkhas, hailing from the hills, are not natural swimmers, and so the troops were apprehensive about getting into the water. Bipin volunteered to go first. Clad in his combat uniform, with his rifle and backpack on his back and a thick rope tied around his waist, he swam across the nallah, his strong strokes pushing his lithe body forward, against the raging current. He climbed out on the other side with his uniform soaked and boots dripping water. Using one hand to wipe the spray off his face, he untied the rope wound around his waist and secured it to a tree trunk. The other end of the rope was being held by the Gorkha troops on the other bank, who then tied it up and got into the water one by one and swam across the canal, using the rope for support against the fast flow of the water.

'Bipin was a good swimmer. He was quick to volunteer for the task. I saw him swimming across the canal with the rope tied around his waist, after which the rest of us crossed over. His courage was immediately recognized by the Gorkha troops, known for their own fortitude,' remembers Gen. Sharma. 'He did very well in whatever event he participated in. When he took the unit for a mine-laying comp, we came first or second, I am forgetting exactly what, but we did superbly well. He subsequently topped almost all his courses.'

## Taking a Convoy to Uttarkashi

In 1982, the dynamic Lt Col Abjeet Mamik took over 5/11 GR, and the young Captains got to serve with their third Commanding Officer. Col Mamik would have a deep influence on both Bipin and Rakesh, and Mrs Bubbles Mamik looked upon the two of them as her own boys.

Soon, the unit received move orders to Harsil, an army cantonment on the banks of the Bhagirathi River in Uttarkashi district of Uttarakhand, just 100 km from the China border. Rakesh handed over the Adjutant's charge to Bipin and moved out as Officer Commanding (OC), Advance Party. Bipin came to Dehradun with the unit on the army special train, from where he took a convoy to Uttarkashi, which was about 78 km from Harsil. In winters, the unit stationed at Harsil would come down to Bhatwari, since it would start snowing and temperatures would dip below freezing point. In summers, they would move back to Harsil.

For Bipin, it was a homecoming of sorts, since his mother belonged to Thati, a small village in Uttarkashi. He and Rakesh made a trip to Thati during the tenure, and the elders in the village were delighted to see that the six-month-old baby with fat pink cheeks, whom they had last seen in his mother's lap more than two decades back, had grown into this strapping young army officer.

One of the high points of Bipin's Harsil tenure was a presentation on contemporary China in early 1982 that he and Rakesh jointly made for the entire command at Joshimath. While the two of them were keynote speakers, Col Mamik acted as their moderator.

'Part of that show was about the '62 war, but largely it was about how China was changing,' remembers Gen. Sharma. 'Col Mamik made us sit down and read books on China that he had got for us from Delhi. Both of us would meticulously go through these, make detailed notes in pencil, exchange ideas, script our presentations, make corrections. It inculcated in us the habit of reading, which continued all our lives.'

Much to Col Mamik's satisfaction, his two youngsters worked really hard, burnt the midnight oil, and the show turned out to be a phenomenal hit.

Sixteen years later, in 1998, when Col Rakesh Sharma was commanding 5/11 GR in Binnaguri and Bipin was his Second-in-Command, the two of them again made a similar presentation on China, which too received praise at the highest level. 'Thanks to these two literary events, our information about China was really detailed, not just in terms of border disputes but also in terms of their politics. In fact, we had been exposed to both our neighbours, since we had been at the Pakistan border in Amritsar and at the China border in Harsil,' explains Gen. Sharma. All this in-depth research would lead to a continuing interest in both countries that helped Bipin take informed decisions regarding China as well as Pakistan when he became COAS and later CDS.

## Bogra Day Celebration

Meanwhile, back in December 1982, 5/11 GR organized the inaugural function of Bogra Day, the battalion's Battle Honour. It commemorated one of the fiercest battles of the 1971 war that had been fought by the Gorkhas. Tasked with capturing the strategic town of Bogra in what was then East Pakistan, the unit had managed to achieve the seemingly impossible on the morning of 16 December 1971 through sheer grit and fear instilled in the enemy largely by extensive use of Molotov cocktails (a hand thrown incendiary weapon also called petrol bomb), since the Pakistanis were mortally afraid of death by fire, which they believed would consign them to hell. The same evening, at 4.41 p.m., the Eastern Command of the Pakistan Army signed the surrender agreement. For this phenomenal victory, 5/11 GR were awarded the Battle Honour Bogra and the Theatre Honour East Pakistan. They were also awarded three Vir Chakras: then CO, Lt Col F.T. Dais; Maj. A.S. Mamik; and Maj. J.B.S. Yadava were the recipients.

Lt Gen. F.T. Dias, who had commanded the unit during that battle, was present at the function in 1982, as were Lt Gen. Sushil Kumar, Colonel of the Regiment, and Col Mamik, who happened to be the CO of the unit. It had taken eleven years for the unit to get recognition, and a grand function was organized in Uttarkashi. 'It was a big day for us. We put in all our effort to organize the event, which turned out to be a grand success,' shares Gen. Sharma.

On 3–4 December 2021, Chief of Defence Staff General Bipin Rawat, PVSM, UYSM, AVSM, YSM, SM, VSM, ADC, would be the chief guest at the 5/11 Gorkha Rifles Bogra Day Golden Jubilee celebration in Delhi. He would drink and dance and smile, with his arms around the men he considered his brothers in arms. Four days later, he would be gone in a freak helicopter crash.

# Like Father, Like Son

Mumbai
1983

Every morning at 6 a.m., two smartly turned-out officers from 5/11 GR would report to Col S.K. Jaitley, Commanding Officer of 9 Dogra, the unit located at the beachside US Club. Dressed in their combat uniforms, they would stand by for instructions for training, which would last till 8.30 a.m. and would mostly involve getting familiar with the use of mortars and recoilless rifles.

While Capt. Rakesh Sharma was aide-de-camp (ADC) to Gen. Laxman Singh Rawat (Bipin's father), who was posted in Mumbai, Capt. Bipin Rawat had taken two months' leave and come down from Harsil, where he was serving with his unit. Both friends were being trained for the Battalion Support Weapons (BSW) course, a precursor to the compulsory Junior Command (JC). 'We should have done it earlier, but since the unit could not spare us from Amritsar, we were being sent now. Col Jaitley was giving us a pre-course training,' recollects Gen. Sharma, time-travelling back to his days as a young Captain. After their sixty-day pre-training had ended, both officers were sent to Mhow for the four-month BSW course, and much to Gen. Laxman Singh Rawat's satisfaction, both returned with wide smiles and 'Instructor' grades.

When Rakesh was still at Harsil, Gen. Rawat had asked him if he would like to come to Mumbai as his ADC. Bipin had urged him to take on the appointment. '*Arre, sir, jao,*' he had insisted, and Rakesh had agreed. In the years that followed, Rakesh had started looking upon the Rawats as his own family. Bipin was already a good friend; now he got to know Gen. and Mrs Rawat better too. He was ADC for three and a half years, and became like a son to them, to the extent that when Gen. Rawat was losing his memory in the latter days of his life, he would call out for Rakesh repeatedly, saying, '*Sharma kahan hai* (Where is Sharma)?' and would demand to know why Rakesh hadn't come to see him.

'I received a lot of affection from them,' acknowledges Gen. Sharma. He says both he and his wife were privileged to learn from the exemplary qualities of the Rawat couple and to witness the fine bond that existed between Bipin and his parents.

'Gen. Laxman Rawat was a great man,' he says. 'Both he and Mrs Sushila Rawat had great honour and integrity, and were almost saintly in their attitude towards life. I have served with many Generals but never felt anyone coming close to them in my entire career.'

Gen. Sharma says he never saw Gen. Rawat lose his temper. 'He was calm, collected, focused, dedicated to his work and had an uprightness that had passed down to Bipin as well. Bipin had imbibed the culture of his parents. He displayed exactly the same moral character as his father.'

Gen. Sharma says that in the following years, when he worked closely with Bipin Rawat, he often saw reflections of the father in the son. 'In matters of honour and integrity, Bipin was the same as his parents. They would treat anyone who approached them with respect and so would Bipin. Even when he was Vice Chief and later Chief, with a dozen important issues playing on his mind, there was never an instance of anyone having to wait for taking an appointment with him. If someone wanted to meet him, he was always available. We never heard from his office, "Chief busy *hain*."'

In fact, on what was to be the last day of their lives, Gen. and Mrs Rawat were leaving their house for the airport when the recently retired Subedar Major of 5/11 GR dropped by to meet them. Despite being in a hurry, the couple stopped to talk to the SM and his wife, and took out time for a photograph as well. That remains the last picture of the couple.

Just like his father, Bipin also genuinely cared about people. 'There were instances when Bipin would be crossing a Defence Security Corps soldier on duty and would just stop by for a moment to ask, "*Haan, kya haal hai bacche? Sab theek hai* (Yes, how are you, kid? Everything all right)?" A soldier limping by would catch his attention. "*Kya ho gaya, langda ke kyun chal raha hai* (What happened? Why are you limping)?" he would ask, genuinely concerned about the welfare of the men serving with him. He also did not make any unnecessary demands on anyone. He would never want to disturb a senior officer on his visits, always insisting that even a soldier or a youngster could be detailed to brief him or accompany him on official assignments. He firmly believed in being accessible and letting everyone have an opportunity to speak and interact with him. He was as much a soldier's Chief as he was an officer's. These were the qualities he had learnt from his parents, both of whom were extremely grounded people,' says Gen. Sharma.

## Moist Eyes at Sister's Wedding

Gen. and Mrs Rawat's daughter, Kiran, Bipin's younger sister, got married in 1985. The groom, Bikram, was the son of Brig. Nathu Singh, former Director General, Ordnance. It was an arranged marriage. A meeting between Kiran and Bikram had been organized in Mumbai, where Kiran's father had been posted. She had been doing medicine from Jammu Medical College, while Bikram had been working in the US. By the time the marriage was fixed, Gen. Rawat had moved to Bhatinda as General Commanding Officer, 10 Corps. Rakesh had accompanied him there as his ADC. He shares some fond memories. 'Kiran got married on 10 March 1985. Since the Corps was still coming up, General and Mrs Rawat were staying in a three-bedroom Major's accommodation in the cantonment. The house had a big lawn, and that was where the wedding took place.'

Bipin, then a Captain, took leave and came to Bhatinda for his sister's wedding. He and Rakesh were tasked with driving down to Hisar to receive the *baraat*, following true Indian hospitality customs. They started early and took turns at the wheel, reaching the ITDC hotel, where lunch had been organized well in time. The baraat came from Delhi—the groom's family lived in Green Park. The two young officers received them courteously and looked after them. 'Since Bipin was serving in Harsil, and I had been with his parents in Bhatinda, I knew the groom's side better than he did. I had even been to Green Park with Gen. Rawat in the days when the marriage was being finalized,' says Gen. Sharma with a laugh.

The two of them then escorted the baraat back to Bhatinda, where the guests were put up in the National Thermal Power Corporation guest rooms and at a hotel outside the cantonment that had been booked for them. The *pheras* were conducted at the Rawat residence, where Rakesh watched Bipin getting emotional at his sister's *vidai*, though trying his best to hide it. 'Bipin was a sentimental man but did not usually show it. When Kiran was leaving, he had tears in his eyes,' remembers Gen. Sharma.

The most remarkable thing about Kiran's wedding was that despite being in a position of privilege, Gen. Rawat was certain that he would not take any favours from the army: 'My daughter is getting married. I shall pay for everything. I don't want to take anything from the Corps.' Though the accommodation was expensive, every bill, every penny was accounted for and paid by Gen. Rawat. 'It was such a great learning for Bipin and me.' In fact, when Gen. Bipin Rawat was COAS and his elder daughter, Kittu, got married, he faithfully followed his father's example. He did exactly the same thing as his father had done: No army facilities were used. The entire baraat was put up at the Lemon Tree Hotel in Delhi, and Bipin paid every single bill.

Bipin was also very close to his parents and siblings. Theirs was a simple, close-knit family. That was true for his own family as well, when he married the lovely Madhulika and they had two beautiful daughters. While he was on his postings, Madhu and their two daughters moved in with his parents at their Noida home. The gentle and considerate Madhu looked after her ailing mother-in-law and later her father-in-law when he started suffering from dementia. When the disease got worse, Bipin took Gen. Laxman Rawat along to Uri, where he was serving as General Officer Commanding, 19th Infantry Division. His younger brother Vijay's son also stayed with Madhulika when he was doing his graduation from Amity College, Noida. He later went on to join 5/11 Gorkha Rifles.

In a happy coincidence, many years later, when Rakesh got posted as Brigadier General Staff (BGS) 10 Corps and came to Bhatinda, he was allotted the same house that General and Mrs Rawat had stayed in during Kiran's wedding. Bipin visited the Sharmas in that phase and stayed with them to revive old memories.

*Crash site*
*8 December 2021*
*Around 12.30 p.m.*

*The helicopter keeps burning. Massive red flames lick the misty sky, cutting through the translucent haze. There are more blasts. 'We carried large pots and kept pouring water, but we couldn't go too close. It was too hot,' says Raja, a sanitation worker with the Coonoor Panchayat.*

*Rescue operations are hampered since the crash has taken place in the middle of a forest replete with thorny bushes, nearly 6 km away from the closest road. It takes almost ten minutes for people from around the area to start collecting at the crash site. A labourer, also named Raja, gets a call from his friend in Kattery and reaches the spot in ten minutes. 'We saw a person who was on fire but alive,' he says. 'He waved his hand like he was calling for help. So my friends and I pulled him out and used a bedsheet to carry him up the hill to the road.'*

# 'I'm Here with a Marriage Proposal'

Tons Valley
Indian Military Academy
Dehradun
Summer of 1985

Twenty-seven-year-old Captain Bipin Rawat, instructor at the Army Cadet College, is deeply engrossed in a weapons-training class he is taking when he notices that the attention of his cadets is straying. About to give them a piece of his mind, he stops speaking, feels a presence behind him and turns to see who it is. Lt Vijay Rawat, the notorious Chhotu, his younger brother, stands there with his hands in the pockets of his pants, grinning from ear to ear.

'What are you doing here?' Bipin asks him curtly. 'Aren't you supposed to be at MCEME [the Military College of Electronics and Mechanical Engineering, Secunderabad]?'

'I'm here with a marriage proposal for you, Bunny,' Vijay shoots back, waving an envelope in the air. '*Photo bhi hai. Dikhaun* (There's a photo as well. Wanna see)?'

An embarrassed Bipin hopes the cadets have not heard it. 'I am busy right now. You go and wait in my room,' he whispers. 'I'll come there as soon as my class gets over.'

With that he hands over a key to Vijay, telling him to go to Collin's Block, and turns his attention back to the cadets, who have noticed the physical similarity between the two and are placing bets that they are brothers.

'Collin's Block now houses only cadets, but back then, a wing was reserved for staff quarters, and that was where Bipin was staying,' says Vijay, remembering how he acted as the messenger boy when Madhulika's proposal came for his brother. 'I was doing my degree course at MCEME, and we had our summer break, so I was on my way to Dehradun. Dad was serving as Corps Commander, 10 Corps, in Bhatinda, but happened to be in Delhi for some work. Since I was crossing Delhi, he'd asked me to come see him.'

It was around the same time that Madhulika's father had proposed a match between his daughter and Bipin. Gen. Rawat liked the proposal and had written a detailed letter to Bipin, giving details about the girl and her family. He wanted Vijay to take the letter to Dehradun and hand it over to Bipin, along with a photograph of the girl.

Vijay took the sealed envelope and boarded a Delhi Transport Corporation bus to Dehradun at the Inter-State Bus Terminal. 'Being an officer and a gentleman, I resisted all temptation to open it,' he says. 'I went to Nanaji's 14 New Road bungalow, and the very next day, after a hefty breakfast, I took a shared autorickshaw from Jhanda Chowk. It dropped me off at the gates of the Indian Military Academy.'

When Bipin got back to his room during the lunch break, Vijay handed him the letter from their father, egging his brother on to open it. A self-conscious Bipin slit open the envelope, and a picture tumbled out. It was a colour photograph of a pretty girl wearing a sari and an endearing smile.

'If you like the girl, take a day's leave and come to Delhi. You both can meet and talk and take a decision,' Gen. Rawat had written, leaving the choice of further action with Bipin. His job done, Vijay left. After his vacation got over, he went back to Secunderabad to complete his degree.

Bipin liked the girl. She was Madhulika Raje Singh, the twenty-two-year-old daughter of Mrigendra Singh, the riyasatdar of the Sohagpur riyasat in Shahdol district of Madhya Pradesh. Her father was also a Congress MLA from the district in 1967 and 1972. Madhu had done her schooling from Gwalior's Scindia Kanya Vidyalaya and then moved to Delhi, where she studied psychology at Daulat Ram College.

There had been no dearth of proposals for Gen. Laxman Singh Rawat's son Bipin, an eligible bachelor and a handsome Captain in the army who came from a renowned family of Garhwal. But it was fate that brought Madhu and Bipin together. Bipin's mother's family had been close to the owners of Banjara Estate in Dehradun. They had a daughter-in-law named Prabha Devi, who belonged to Rewa district of Madhya Pradesh. Prabha's father happened to be a friend of Madhulika's father. Prabha was the one who suggested Bipin as a match for Madhulika.

Bipin and Madhu liked each other's photographs, and a meeting was set up between them. Many years later, Madhu talked to Col Satpal Parmar, Bipin's maternal uncle, about that first meeting with her future husband. She laughingly admitted that both she and Bipin were so shy that other than an exchange of very formal 'hellos' and 'how are yous', the two had no conversation that day. However, they both liked each other and conveyed acceptance to their respective fathers. Since the families already approved of the match, the marriage was fixed for 14 April 1986.

## A Perfect Match between Two Simple People

13 April 1986
Bhatinda

A few private cars and a busload of *baraatis* were slowly making their way from Bhatinda, Punjab, to Delhi. They were on their way to the Kanishka hotel, where arrangements had been made for their stay. The marriage venue was 25 Ashok Road, a large bungalow rented by Madhulika's family. The bus stopped at a resort near Sirsa for lunch.

'Since my brother was getting married, I was really excited. I had organized some cases of beer and some bottles of Scotch for my cousins,' remembers Vijay.

But Gen. Rawat, knowing his younger son's reputation for mischief, had deliberately not made him in-charge of the liquor quota, which was being handled by the responsible and reliable Capt. Rakesh Sharma, who was Gen. Rawat's ADC.

The baraatis reached the hotel in the evening, where Vijay and his cousins immediately got down to the serious business of drinking. 'Since I wanted to save my own liquor, I went across to Capt. Sharma and said, "Sir, *kuch bottle Scotch de do* (Give us some bottles of Scotch),' Vijay confesses with a laugh.

Rakesh handed one bottle to him with a stern, '*Bas, ab aur nahi milegi* (No more).'

Vijay made a sad face and got back to his gang. 'I already had two bottles, so all of us sat in one of the rooms and had a party. We ordered some food and had a good time. Around midnight, we went down to the lobby and roamed around,' he says.

When he got back to Bhatinda after the wedding, Sushila Rawat, who had not gone in the baraat, called him to her room. 'Mom had heard that we had got drunk and were roaming in the hotel lobby, and she gave me a solid piece of her mind,' Vijay says.

A self-conscious Bipin was brought for the *haldi* ceremony the next morning, and around 7 p.m., the baraat left for the marriage venue, which was quite close to the hotel.

'I recollect my sister Kiran was so decked up that guests in the hotel thought she was the bride and wanted pictures taken with her. We had to tell them that she was not the bride but the groom's sister, and drag her away,' shares Vijay.

Gen. Bipin Rawat ('Bunny') was a chubby, smiling baby whom everyone adored. When his parents took him to the village for the first time, the household helps would fight over who would hold him first.

Bunny was always a caring elder brother to his sibling Chhotu (later Col Vijay Rawat), who was always up to some mischief.

All dressed up for a fancy-dress party. Later in life, he hardly cared about clothes, leaving the choice to his buddies or his wife.

Wearing the Gurkha *topi* and *khukri* many years before he actually went on to join 5/11 Gorkha Rifles as a young Second Lieutenant.

The quiet, softspoken Gentleman Cadet Bipin Rawat at the Indian Military Academy, Dehradun.

The Gentleman Cadet in his winter patrol.

Indian Military Academy, passing-out ceremony: The quiet, reticent Gentleman Cadet whom nobody knew passed out as the Sword of Honour.

At the IMA passing-out: Flanked by his maternal uncle, then Maj. Satpal Parmar, whom he remained very close to all his life; and his grandfather's younger brother, Thakur Kishan Singh, at whose Dehradun house Bipin spent most of his vacations.

At his passing-out, flanked by the proud ladies of the family and his maternal uncle, then Maj. Satpal Parmar. His mother stands between him and Maj. Parmar.

In the hot seat.

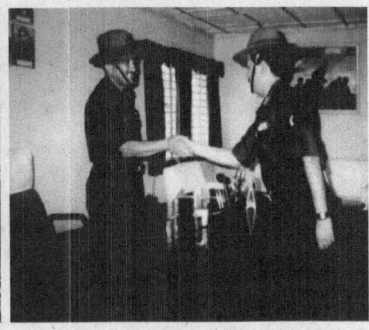

One tiger handing over the reins to the next: Col Rakesh Sharma hands over command of 5/11 GR to then Lt Col Bipin Rawat.

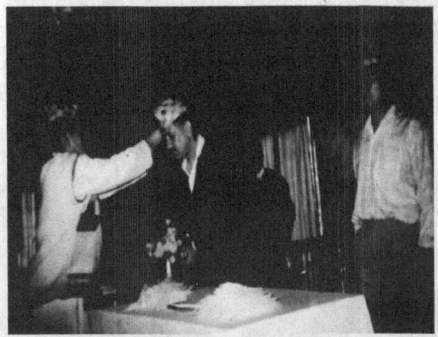

The unit panditji doing the *tika* after the Dussehra puja at Binnaguri in 1999 while then Subedar Major Kumar Pradhan looks on.

Reliving the CO and SM Sahab bond: With retired Subedar Major Kumar Pradhan (who was SM of 5/11 Gorkha Rifles during his command), at his residence after he took over as COAS.

The *shastra* puja (arms worship, part of the nine-day Dussehra celebrations) at Binnaguri in 1998, when he was commanding 5/11 GR.

Tiger on the prowl: Visiting the Alfa Company post at Dichu, Arunachal Pradesh.

With the then governor of Arunachal Pradesh.

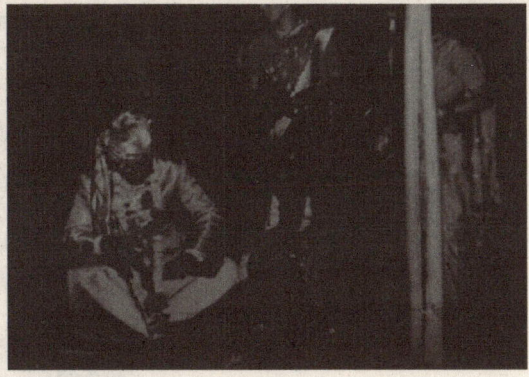

Bipin and Madhulika got married in a simple ceremony.

Farewell to the bachelor days: While he was sitting for the *pheras*, his shoes got stolen.

The newly-weds caught in a candid shot.

Photogenic smiles marking the beginning of a beautiful journey together.

A warm send-off from the regiment after relinquishing command. He was adored by his men.

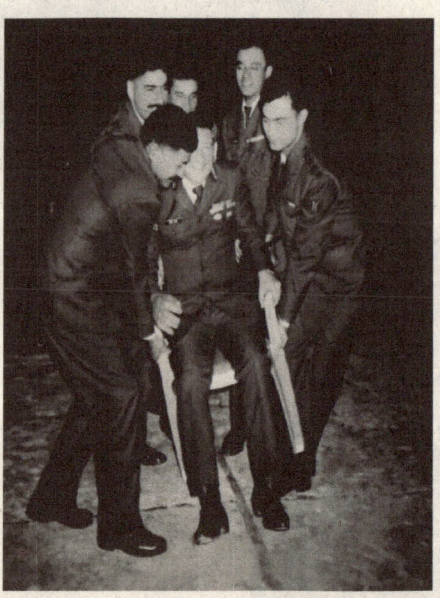

He's a jolly good fellow, and so say all of us: End of tenure as Commanding Officer.

On a visit to 5/11 Gorkha Rifles in Lucknow: He always had a warm handshake and a pleasant greeting for all his soldiers and officers.

Though he shot up like a meteor, Gen. Rawat remained deeply attached to his unit. Visiting 5/11 GR, as a Brigadier, in Jammu and Kashmir.

In the colourful Gorkhali topi his troops loved to see him in.
He spoke fluent Gorkhali too.

He was happiest with his troops and could do the Nepali
dance jhamre as well as the youngest soldier.

The higher he rose in rank, the more grounded he became:
Happy with the Gorkha troops.

With his IMA course mate Maj. Gen. Arjun Muthanna in Kodagu on 4 November 2017, where Gen. Rawat unveiled the statues of two iconic soldiers of the district: Field Marshal K.M. Cariappa and Gen. K.S. Thimayya.

Gen. Rawat was known for his firm handshake, and he looked deep into people's eyes. He seldom wore dark glasses. Visiting 5/11 GR at Umroi Cantt during his Corps Commander days.

As Corps Commander in Dimapur, cutting a handsome figure in his Six Bravo (summer mess attire), with the charming Madhulika.

In a locally woven Naga jacket as Corps Commander.

The baton passes on: Gen. Bipin Rawat took over as the Indian Army's twenty-sixth Chief of the Army Staff from General Dalbir Singh Suhag, PVSM, UYSM, AVSM, VSM, ADC, on 31 December 2016. (*Left to right*): Namita Suhag, Gen. Suhag, Gen. Rawat and Madhulika Rawat.

Chief of the Army Staff and the first lady with Param Vir Chakra awardee Company Quartermaster Havildar Abdul Hamid's wife, Rasoolan Bibi.

As COAS on a visit to St Petersburg, Russia.

As COAS on a visit to Bhutan.

A proud day for the family, December 1982. Then Capt. Bipin Rawat and his parents came to Dehradun for the passing-out parade of 2Lt Vijay Rawat. (*Left to right*): then Capt. Bipin Rawat, Gen. Laxman Singh Rawat, 2Lt Vijay Rawat and Sushila Rawat.

The three siblings with their respective partners, at a family get-together at Kiran's Delhi house. Gen. Bipin Rawat was Army Commander at that time. (*Left to right*): Gen. Bipin Rawat, Madhulika, Vikram Singh (brother-in-law), Kiran (sister), Col Vijay Rawat (brother) and Sanyogita (sister-in-law).

Gen. Rawat ran into his class teacher Mrs Gunmala Singh from St Edward's School, Shimla, at a party and recognized her right away.

Diplomatic evening overseas: Madhulika and Gen. Rawat with Geetika and Brig. Lidder in Kazakhstan, at a royal banquet held in their honour in August 2017.

A Europe trip: The Rawats and the Lidders in Prague, November 2021. Happy and smiling, unmindful of the terrible tragedy that was to befall.

Gen. Rawat with his National Defence Academy course mate Lt Gen Subrata Saha. The two of them had known each other since they were seventeen-year-olds.

With Gen. Naravane in Panagarh for Corps War Game.

Pinning the badge: 'Impress me with work, not gifts,' Gen. Rawat would often say. Gen. Naravane says the only gift he ever gave Gen. Rawat was a Naga spear broach that he had pinned on his jacket in Kohima during a visit in 2014.

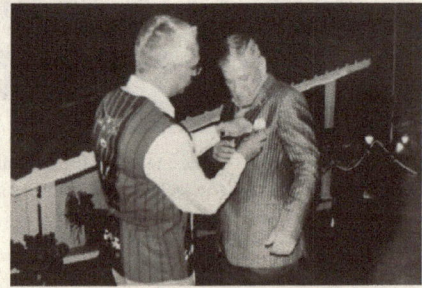

Lt Gen. Lakshman Singh Rawat flanked by Gen. Bipin Rawat, Col Satpal Parmar and Brig. Shivender Singh at L.S. Rawat's flat in Noida.

'*Hum sab bhi fauj mein jayenge. It will be a tribute to Mausaji,*' a teenaged Bipin had told his cousin Shivender when Shivender's father died in the 1971 war. Here they stand in their uniforms many years later, in Pir Ki Gali, Kashmir, where Gen. Rawat had gone to visit his cousin.

He was an affectionate father to his daughters. Tarini (*left*), the younger one, and Kritika, the older one.

The Rawats at their elder daughter Kritika's wedding reception in Mumbai.

The baton passes on to the twenty-seventh Chief of the Army Staff, Gen. Manoj Mukund Naravane.

The baton changes hands. Gen. Naravane says Gen. Rawat groomed him for the job without saying a single word to him.

The author in conversation with Gen. Rawat when she visited his office to gift him a copy of her book *Kargil*.

Tarini remembering her parents with a smile at an interview with the author at Tarini's house in Delhi.

The Chief of the Army Staff meeting the long-haired Saransh and assuring him that it was perfectly all right to choose a career option other than the army.

The President and supreme commander of the Indian armed forces, Ram Nath Kovind, conferring the PVSM on Gen. Bipin Rawat

A rare photograph of India's top military men, the tri-service Chiefs, accompanied by the first ladies.

The tri-service Chiefs and first ladies in casual attire.

The last picture of the Rawats, taken on 8 December 2021, with Sub. Maj. Bhishma Shreshta of 5/11 GR, just before they left for the Palam air base to take a flight to Sulur.

Bipin wore a cream-coloured sherwani, with some golden embroidery on it, and an elegant *safa*. He made the perfect contrast to Madhulika, who was dressed in a beautiful red *lehenga*. During the *jaimala*, Bipin had Vijay whispering fiercely in his ear, '*Pair mat kheenchne dena, joote mat utaarne dena* (Don't let anyone take off your shoes).' But despite Vijay's constant vigil, the girls from Madhulika's family managed to hide Bipin's shoes when he took them off while sitting for the *pheras*.

'I think I was distracted looking for whisky when that happened,' Vijay jokes. 'I don't know how much he gave for the shoes. He didn't tell me.'

The wedding ceremony went on through the night, and after the pheras got over, early morning around 4 a.m., the close family returned to the hotel.

When Vijay got back to his room, he was surprised to find someone already asleep in his bed. It turned out to be Capt. (later Gen.) Surinder Mehta, his own course mate. Mehta had joined 5/11 GR and had been sent to officially represent the unit at Bipin's wedding.

'He had reached so late that he missed the wedding and was so tired that he just fell asleep on my bed,' says Vijay. 'When Mehta saw me glaring at him, he woke up and offered to sleep on the sofa, but I told him not to bother since I had to go back to Bhabhi's place for a puja after taking a bath.'

After breakfast, the baraat left for Bhatinda with the beautiful bride and the delighted groom, where an eager Sushila Rawat was waiting to receive them with a traditional puja. A few days later, a simple reception was held in Bhatinda, at the residence of the GOC (where the Rawats' daughter, Kiran, had also got married), and Madhulika was introduced to Bipin's friends and family. Gentle and caring by temperament, she immediately became a favourite with everyone. Not only was she an understanding partner to Bipin, but she was also a loving mother to their two daughters, Kritika and Tarini, and a very devoted daughter to her in-laws. She stayed with them in their Noida house after Gen. Laxman

Singh Rawat retired and nursed them in their old age, continuing to be by their side till the time they passed away.

It was only after these responsibilities had been taken care of that she went to stay with Bipin and took on the mantle of the first lady with grace and charm. She was by his side as he rose in rank and service and took over the highest appointments in the Indian Army.

## Madhulika

Madhulika or Madhu or Muddy—as her closest friends from school called her—was a sweet girl. Though she came from an illustrious family and was married to the highest-ranking officer in the Indian defence forces, she continued to be her humble, grounded self, which was something she had in common with her famous husband.

'Both Muddy and Bipin were really simple people,' says Sonal Bole, one of Madhulika's best friends from Scindia. The two had been friends ever since they were ten-year-olds, having taken admission in the fourth standard. Sonal remembers Madhu as a happy, bubbly girl who loved needlework and hated maths. 'She would get along with everybody, and even when Bipin became Army Chief, she remained the same friendly person. We would all be welcome to her house,' says Sonal.

## The Quiet, Smiling Bipin

She remembers staying at Army House with her childhood friend. They would get chikki and khakra for Bipin, who would keep the snacks in jars by his bedside, since he was fond of midnight snacks when he was working. At dinnertime she, Madhu and Tarini would sit at the dinner table in their pyjamas and sweatshirts, with a smiling Bipin turning up in his formal shirts and trousers.

'Bipin did not speak much. He would just smile when we pestered him with, "Bipin, tell *na*, what's happening between India and Pakistan,"' Sonal says.

She remembers one particular occasion when Bipin spoke about Prime Minister Narendra Modi with great regard. At their daughter Kritika's wedding reception in Mumbai, Bipin and Madhu were sitting at the same table as Sonal and her husband. Bipin mentioned a flight he had recently taken, with the prime minister and the agriculture minister both on board. 'He said that PM Modi took a forty-five-minute nap on the aircraft, had a meeting with the agriculture minister and then a meeting with Bipin, back to back. Bipin said that the prime minister was completely updated on what points he wanted to discuss, had full faith in Bipin's viewpoint and left the decision-making completely to Bipin, saying that as Army Chief Bipin obviously knew best. Bipin was very appreciative of this completely professional attitude in a political leader,' says Sonal.

Sonal also remembers how proud Bipin was of his troops. 'He said that the Indian Army is made of brave men who will give their lives for their country, but the world is advancing very fast, and future wars will not be fought on the ground but more in terms of technology, which is why we need technological upgrades.' That was one of the rare occasions when Bipin sat down at leisure and spoke about his profession, Sonal admits, since he was always very busy.

'Madhu was really excited about the house they were planning to build in Dehradun, where they wanted to shift to after his retirement. But they did not plan to take anything from the official residence,' Sonal says. 'In fact, Madhu had shown me how Bipin had got all the furniture in Army House stamped, so that it always stayed in Army House and could not be pilfered at any point of time.'

She also recounts how Bipin had cut down extra expenditure at Army House, starting with the Army Day lunch that was traditionally hosted by the Army Chief. 'Till then the food would be catered from a five-star hotel and would cost around Rs 1500 per person, but after Bipin took over, he said that instead of hotels the lunch would be catered by the army mess. He was really pleased when the per-person expenditure came down to a third of what it had cost earlier. It became a "for the Army, by the Army" event.'

According to Sonal, Madhulika was nervous about being a senior officer's wife in the army. 'She did not enjoy stardom. Even Bipin didn't. They were earthy people, not socialites, and Muddy would often say that her husband was "married to the country".'

'Muddy was a good human being, a loving friend, a devoted wife and daughter-in-law, and a caring mother,' says Sonal. 'She will always be missed.'

# Dancing on a Plastered Leg, under the Enemy's Nose

8 December 2021
Secunderabad

Col Durga Prasad was about to sit down for lunch when he saw a message flash on his cell phone. 'Bipin's helicopter has gone missing,' someone had posted on the 5/11 Gorkha Rifles WhatsApp group. A shocked Durga opened the chat to find that officers were responding to the message. Apparently, the news was all over the media. He walked over to the television set and switched it on. Images of Bipin Rawat were flashing on the screen: happy, smiling, proud in his Gorkha hat and uniform. Col Durga's mind was diving into its own bank of memories. He remembered a younger Bipin, in the same hat, smiling that same slightly lop-sided smile many years back.

\* \* \*

October 1987
Uri
Jammu and Kashmir
5/11 GR battalion location

Unit adjutant and Alfa Company commander Maj. Bipin
Rawat is limping forward with a purposeful glint in his eye, a
stick supporting the weight falling on his plastered foot. Lt Col
Durga Prasad, officiating Commanding Officer, looks at him
warily. Dussehra celebrations have just got over, and Durga is
planning to retire to his room for a desperately needed siesta—
brought on by beer, a big lunch and some vigorous, high-energy
foot-shaking.

'Sir, I have to go and celebrate Dussehra with my company
boys,' Bipin says, as enthusiastic as a schoolboy. Durga looks at
Bipin's plastered foot. He had cracked his ankle during a walk a
few days back and had been advised complete bedrest by the unit
doctor, with instructions to be on six weeks of sick leave, since he
was temporarily 'Low Medical Category' and not fit to serve in the
forward area. Bipin had refused outright and, instead, submitted
a signed affidavit saying he was staying back in Uri against the
doctor's advice, at his own risk. And now, he wanted to go up to
Chakothi, the Alfa Company post, much ahead and right on the
Indo–Pakistan border.

'No, you can't go,' Durga tells him, pointing towards the injured
foot. 'You can't even walk properly. How will you climb?'

'Arre, sir! Please, permission *de do*. I will handle everything,'
Bipin pleads. He keeps pleading and cajoling till Durga finally
gives way. At last light, around 5 p.m., the 5/11 jazz band, two
Nepali singers and a pleased Bipin pile on a one-tonne truck and,
with headlights switched off, drive away on the road that leads to
Chakothi and is under direct enemy observation. They reach the
road head, where the vehicle is parked, in about forty-five minutes.
Thereafter, it is a 6 km uphill climb to the post, where the Jhelum

River enters India from Pakistan, and the two neighbours sit with their guns aimed at each other.

News has reached the *kanchas*, who are thrilled to know that their Company Commander is on his way to meet them. Some of them have come down to the road. They carry Bipin up to the post in the true Gorkha spirit of '*Ho ki hoina? Ho! Ho! Ho!* (Is he the greatest or not? Yes, he is! Yes, he is! Yes, he is!)'

'With the jazz band playing Nepali songs, and the boys singing and dancing right under the Pakistanis' trained guns, he celebrated Dusshera with his company,' recounts a nostalgic Col Durga Prasad, sitting in his Secunderabad home. 'We were face to face with Pakistan on that post, but luckily they were so intimidated by the formidable Gorkha reputation of cutting heads off with *khukris* that they did not initiate any firing.'

At 1 a.m. the next day, Bipin was back, very pleased with himself and happy to have met the men he loved so much. 'He was like that,' Col Durga remembers with an affectionate smile. 'Once he set his mind to something, he would just go ahead and do it.'

## A Quick Trip to Vaishno Devi

Col Durga recounts an evening in Khasa, Amritsar. It was a Friday evening. Bipin, as a young Second Lieutenant on his first posting, was a few drinks down and decided he was going to Vaishno Devi the next morning. He asked all the bachelors drinking with him if anyone would accompany him, but they all refused to be a part of the crazy plan.

'He kept on trying to make us change our minds. And finally, I told him I would come with him, not because I was religious but because I wouldn't let him do it alone,' says Col Durga.

The next morning, the two got into their civvies and left the cantonment at dawn. They hitched a ride in an auto rickshaw to the Amritsar bus stand, took a bus to Jammu, then a jeep to Katra and started walking up to the temple by the shorter but tougher route around 11 p.m. They reached the temple, did their darshan and then walked back through the night, again by the difficult route, and took a jeep taxi to Jammu.

'We went to a unit officer's house there, had drinks and a good hearty lunch, and then boarded a civil bus to Amritsar,' says Col Durga. They reached their rooms late at night and were present for the Monday morning PT parade at 6 a.m.

'People couldn't believe that we had done Vaishno Devi over the weekend,' he says with a laugh. 'But then, that was Bipin. He had this rock-solid determination and an ability to convince people.'

* * *

On 8 December 2021, over the course of the day, television reporters had announced that there was one survivor in the chopper crash. Col Durga was very hopeful that it would be Bipin. 'Bipin had had a brush with death in Uri too, and had come out of it with his life and spirit intact,' he says. He remembers another stressful afternoon when there had been an accident and he had desperately hoped that Bipin was well.

## IED Explosion in Uri

'This was again Uri, in 1988,' he recounts. 'As officiating CO I had been briefing a visiting General. Bipin was adjutant and was coming down from some forward areas in Navakot to Uri with some documents that needed my signatures. He was also bringing along some boys, who had to proceed on leave. Around 3 p.m., I received the shocking news that there had been an IED explosion, and the one-tonne Bipin was driving down in had been hit,' he says.

After informing the visiting General Officer, Col Durga immediately left for the accident site. He was relieved to find Bipin standing by the damaged vehicle, perfectly hale and hearty, and in complete control of the situation. Two soldiers had received minor splinter injuries, but everyone else was fine.

'I was sure he would survive this too,' Col Durga says. Unfortunately, this time it was not to be.

# 'Zyada Peene Se Sehat Kharab Hoti Hai'

8 December 2021
Ghum, Darjeeling
West Bengal

Seventy-year-old retired Subedar Major (Honorary Captain) Kumar Pradhan was at home. He had just switched on the television and was watching the news when an announcement was made that caused his heart to skip a beat. The newsreader was saying that the helicopter carrying India's Chief of Defence Staff, Gen. Bipin Rawat, Mrs Madhulika Rawat and eleven other defence personnel appeared to have crashed in Tamil Nadu's Coonoor region. Pradhan could not believe his ears.

Kumar Pradhan had been a Naik in the regiment when Bipin Rawat joined as a young Second Lieutenant. He had been on leave when the new sahab had joined, but when he came back he met Rawat Sahab—slim, shy, ramrod straight, with a gentle smile and crewcut hair. He would make special efforts to mingle with the troops, would play troop games with them in the evening, often eat with them in the *langar* (the Other Ranks' kitchen). The men liked him, and he seemed to like them a lot too.

Kumar Pradhan had been the unit Subedar Major when, a few years later, Bipin had returned to the unit as the Second-in-Command (2IC) to then Col Rakesh Sharma, who was commanding. He was now totally in sync with what the battalion was doing and deeply concerned about the welfare of the soldiers. Then he took over the unit: quiet, dignified, patient, seldom raising his voice, conveying displeasure only with the tone of his voice.

But the most prominent memories that kept playing in Kumar Pradhan's mind even as announcements about the crash kept coming in through the day were of Bipin at the *barakhanas* that were hosted in the battalion. He was handsome and would always be smiling, and he would stay back till the last toast was drunk. Visiting the tented enclosures set up by the troops, relishing the mutton they had roasted on a coal fire, drinking heartily each time they filled up his glass with Old Monk rum, cracking jokes with them, dancing the Nepali dance *jhamre*, often better than the youngest Gorkha soldiers—sitting on his haunches and throwing his legs in the air effortlessly, singing aloud to the melodies of popular Nepali songs.

\* \* \*

1998
Binnaguri, West Bengal

Subedar Major Kumar Pradhan's brow was marked with worry lines as he carried the Battle Physical Efficiency Test (BPET) roster to the Commanding Officer's office. He knew that CO Sahab was not going to like it. The unit was due for an administrative inspection soon. The Brigade Commander would be visiting and inspecting everything in the battalion, including the physical fitness of troops. The BPET included a series of physical tests and a 5 km run with a load to determine physical standards. While the soldiers had all done very well in the recently conducted timed run, out of the thirteen Junior Commissioned Officers serving in the unit, only six had managed to reach within the stipulated time. The rest had failed.

When he knocked on the office door and walked in, Pradhan found Bipin Rawat deeply engrossed in a register placed on his table. He looked up at Pradhan's 'Jai Hind, sahab' and, replying to his greeting, asked him to sit down. He then looked straight into Pradhan's eyes and asked, 'Pradhan Sahab, *ek baat bataiye. Hamare JCO sahab log kitna peete hain* (Tell me one thing. How much do our JCOs drink)?' A puzzled Pradhan, who was a teetotaler himself, assured Bipin that most of them drank just two pegs each evening, and he could vouch for it, since they would all sit together in the JCOs mess and have drinks and dinner.

Bipin pushed the register lying in front of him towards Pradhan and asked him to take a look. A shocked Pradhan went through the pages, where it was neatly jotted down how much each man was drinking. According to those records, most JCOs were drinking 7–8 pegs of alcohol every day. Bipin then told Pradhan that he had received the actual drinking details of all JCOs from the Bar NCO, who had told him that the JCOs were drinking secretly during the daytime, or even after dinner, while cleverly hiding this from Subedar Major Pradhan.

'*Ye register le jaiye, aur sahab logon ko bataiye ki itna zyada peene se sehat kharab hoti hai* (Take this register, and tell the sahabs that drinking too much is injurious to health),' Bipin said softly and went back to reading the files placed before him. Pradhan Sahab picked up the register and excused himself.

Remembering the incident nearly twenty-four years later, Pradhan Sahab says he was surprised that CO Sahab did not say a single harsh word to him. He called the JCOs who had been hiding their drinking and spoke sternly to them while informing them that the Commanding Officer was aware of what they were doing. The

JCOs were scared of the punishment that would be meted out to them, but Bipin never mentioned it to anyone thereafter and went about interacting with the JCOs as if he knew nothing.

'It embarrassed them so much that a few stopped drinking alcohol altogether, while the rest cut down on it drastically,' says Pradhan. 'In the next admin inspection, conducted six months later, the results were good. Physical fitness standards had improved, and all the JCOs finished the BPET well in time.' Bipin had achieved what he wanted to without saying one unpleasant word to anyone.

'*Isharon mein baat karta tha Sahab* (He used to only hint at what he wanted),' Pradhan says with a smile, going a bit further back to when Bipin was serving as the 2IC to then Col Rakesh Sharma, who was commanding the unit. 'Rawat Sahab had picked up full Colonel's rank, but he was willing to wait so that he could take over his own battalion.'

Pradhan was Subedar Major with Rakesh Sharma, and he then continued in the same appointment with Bipin when he took over command of 5/11 in 1998. 'He commanded the unit in Binnaguri and then took it to Arunachal, from where I retired in the year 2000 while he was still serving as Commanding Officer. *CO Sahab ne hi mera vidai kiya tha* (CO Sahab gave me the send-off from the regiment),' he says and smiles.

Pradhan remembers Bipin as a man who did not speak much but would think deeply about the welfare of soldiers, and take well-thought-out and sensible decisions. 'He would be concerned about what food the soldiers were getting to eat; if they were getting their leave in time or not; if they were happy. He would often visit the langar and sometimes even eat in the Other Ranks kitchen to keep tabs on the quality of food the soldiers were getting,' he says. And while speaking of food, he shifts to another memory, this one from Arunachal Pradesh.

\* \* \*

1999
Gumba village
Arunachal Pradesh

Col Bipin Rawat, his 2IC, Lt Col Surender Singh Mehta, Subedar Major Kumar Pradhan and the unit doctor are sitting in the village headman's hut. Col Rawat has been visiting all his company posts on the China border. He has climbed up to the Dichu post and is now getting acquainted with the *gaon bura* (head of the village). The hut is dark and musty, and there is a strong stench, which the faujis are not used to.

While the others hesitate to sit down, Bipin makes himself comfortable on the gaon bura's bed, smiling warmly at him. The village headman is very pleased that the Commanding Officer of the unit is visiting him, and, taking out a bottle of locally made liquor from under his bed, he offers it to Bipin, who at once agrees to have a drink.

'The room was very dirty. There was a rotten smell inside. While the rest of us were on the verge of puking, CO Sahab was happily reaching out to take a glass of *madira*,' recollects Pradhan Sahab.

The village headman offers the drink to the others, but all three refuse saying they don't drink. The gaon bura then calls out for milk and pours out a glass, offering it to the others.

'It looked so unhygienic that we couldn't even bring ourselves to hold it, let alone drink it,' says Pradhan Sahab.

So the glass remains untouched. Bipin finishes the drink he has been offered, and while the village headman watches him closely, he reaches out for the glass of milk his men have not touched and drinks it up as well, thanking the old man warmly for his hospitality. The four of them then leave.

Once they are on their own, Bipin tells them they should never refuse any food or drink being offered by the villagers. '*Aap aisa karenge toh un logon ko bura lagega. Aisa nahi karna chahiye* (If you do so, they will feel bad. You mustn't do so),' he says.

The next day he goes on scheduled leave.

'When Sahab came back after twelve days, I found out that he had suffered a bad bout of jaundice and was still recovering from it,' says Pradhan Sahab.

A concerned Kumar Pradhan receives the CO and asks him how he contracted jaundice. Bipin quickly tells him, '*Raaste mein ganda pani pee liya tha* (Had some contaminated water on the way).'

A smiling Pradhan tells him, '*Sahab, ye Gumba ke drinks peene se toh nahi hua* (Are you sure it didn't happen due to those drinks you had in Gumba)?'

Bipin just laughs and waves off the accusation.

*Crash site*
*8 December 2021*

*Emergency services, including the police and fire brigade, and the army, reach the site of the crash and take over rescue work. Eight ambulances and six medical teams from Coimbatore's government and private hospitals are sent to the site, though larger fire engines are not able to access the route easily since there has been a traffic jam, which needs to be cleared.*

*By then, the media has also got wind of the accident. Shocked Indians watch as news reports declare that the crashed helicopter was carrying India's Chief of Defence Staff, General Bipin Rawat, his wife, Madhulika, and twelve others. It had crashed about 10 km from the spot where it was meant to land. Two survivors are initially reported and stated to be in critical state. Though struck by grief, the country hopes that Gen. Bipin Rawat is one of them.*

*Around 1.53 p.m., the Indian Air Force confirms the crash and the presence of CDS Gen. Bipin Rawat on board the chopper.*

# Standing Up for His
# Battalion Commander

8 December 2021
Sankey Road, Bangalore
2 p.m.

It has been a long day. Major General Arjun Muthanna, retired from the army and employed with a private firm in Bangalore, finally gets a breather from his busy morning schedule at work and decides to take a break for lunch. He reaches for his cellphone and is glancing at the WhatsApp messages flashing on the screen when he is jolted out of his chain of thoughts.

'CDS Gen. Bipin Rawat's helicopter crashes in Tamil Nadu,' mentions a message on his course mates' group. Arjun looks at it in disbelief. 'VVIP flights have the best aircraft, and best pilots and crew,' is his first thought. 'This can't happen.' He frantically googles for the news looking for a list of survivors but is unable to find any details.

Placing his cell on the table, Arjun leans back on his chair. His mind is flashing before his eyes a series of memories. Bipin as a Gentleman Cadet at the Indian Military Academy—young, tenacious, his warm brown eyes emanating sincerity. Bipin as a Rashtriya Rifles Sector Commander in Sopore, getting up at the Army Commander's briefing, passionately standing up for his men. Bipin, relaxed and smiling, at their meeting in November 2017, when he had unveiled the statues of the iconic Coorgi soldiers—Field Marshal K.M. Cariappa and Gen. K.S. Thimayya. Arjun closes his eyes and lets the memories come to him, one by one.

\* \* \*

2007
Sopore, Kashmir

Located in Baramulla district of Jammu and Kashmir, Sopore (also known as the apple town of Kashmir) was then a hotbed of terrorist activity. Brig. Arjun Muthanna and Brig. Bipin Rawat, who happened to be IMA course mates, were both serving in Kashmir. 'He was Commander, 5 Sector, Rashtriya Rifles, and I was Commander, 10 Sector, Rashtriya Rifles,' Gen. Muthanna says, remembering the friend he lost.

Rawat's area of responsibility included Sopore, which was also where the Kashmiri separatist leader Syed Ali Shah Geelani, who passed away recently, lived. Arjun himself was in Pattan, south of Sopore. 'A lot of terrorist activity was going on in Sopore at that time,' recollects Gen. Muthanna. 'The local people were supportive of the terrorist movement. Calls for protest bandhs [closures] were well subscribed to, partly because of fear and partly because of the general sentiment, which was in favour of the militants. Anything happened and Gilani would be put under house arrest. Bipin used to go and interact with him a lot and tell us about it later.'

He says he distinctly remembers a conference that took place in northern Kashmir, which both Bipin and he attended. 'It was a normal operational review conducted by the Army Commander, which was being attended by officers of the rank of Brigadier and above. The Northern Army Commander, Corps Commander and Divisional (Rashtriya Rifles Force) Commander were present at the conference. Both Bipin and I were Sector Commanders. Each sector had three–four battalions under it, depending upon deployment. Bipin and I were responsible for the battalions that came under us, and we were reporting to the Kilo Force Commander, Kilo standing for North Kashmir. Since RR was an anti-insurgency force, our task was to counter terrorism and make the life of the local people as close to normal as it was possible under the circumstances,' says Gen. Muthanna.

When the Army Commander stood up to speak, he made a passing refence to the RR unit under which Sopore fell. He wanted to know who the Commanding Officer of the unit was and expressed his dissatisfaction with how things were being conducted in the area. 'There was talk that the Sopore unit was not pulling its weight and that it was not doing all that it could, or should, be doing to keep terrorist activity at a low,' remembers Gen. Muthanna.

The statement had just been made in passing and did not really need to be countered, but Bipin immediately stood up. 'I remember he surprised us all by getting up and speaking up for his Commanding Officer. He took the trouble to list out the peculiarities of the area and how well the unit was performing under those circumstances. He put across his point very strongly and explained why he felt that this particular Commanding Officer was doing an excellent job, to the extent that finally the Army Commander said, "Okay, I take this point, and I would like to meet the Commanding Officer." Which he did subsequently,' Gen. Muthanna recounts.

The CO of the Sopore unit was summoned to the next briefing and made a detailed presentation on how he was handling the situation. And finally, the Army Commander went away satisfied with the efforts being made. Gen. Muthanna says the reason why he wishes to highlight this point is that he wants to establish that it was very easy for Bipin to keep quiet that day, but he did not let anyone cast aspersions on his officer's sincerity. 'His reaction deserves mention because as a Brigadier, the Army Commander was three levels higher up for us. You needed courage of conviction to stand up to him and make a point that differed from his.' He adds that Bipin not only made sure that the Army Commander heard him out, but he also put across his point so eloquently and convincingly that the senior officer listened and was eventually convinced.

'It was a great example of a Brigade Commander standing up for his Battalion Commander. He had the ability to not only make the other person see his point of view but also be convinced about it,' Gen. Muthanna states.

## 'He Never Mentioned That His Father Was a Serving Brigadier'

Arjun and Bipin were course mates at the Indian Military Academy. 'Bipin's father was a serving Brigadier, but Bipin never made much of it. He was just another Gentleman Cadet mucking around with the rest of us. He was seen as a hard-working cadet, a good team player and someone who would just put his head down and do what had to be done.'

Gen. Muthanna says he had a lot of affection and respect for his course mate, but he did not agree with a few of the CDS's controversial statements. As an example, he quotes the ruling that officers would have to stay in service guestrooms and not hotels.

In 2018, the army laid down a list of strict dos and don'ts for its officers, in a drive to bring down the running costs. This included orders for officers to use army guestrooms and not hotels when on temporary duty or visits. While interacting with officers in Nashik, Gen. Bipin Rawat was quoted as saying that this would help in curbing corruption. Naming one particular department of the Ministry of Defence that comprises army engineers and civilians, he'd said that there was a possibility that officers staying in hotels may indulge in corrupt practices like 'exchanging briefcases with contractors'.

'I understand the reasoning behind asking officers to stay in service guestrooms, but to say that this was being done to curb corruption was not correct,' Gen. Muthanna says. 'And making a comment like that was completely unfounded and painful, as it literally painted all with the same brush of corruption.'

* * *

On 8 December 2021, everyone in Gen. Rawat's course mates' group was shocked at the news and was waiting to know if there were any survivors. But by evening it was clear that all but one had succumbed. 'My first thought was that Bipin had been in one crash too many—considering his providential escape in his previous helicopter crash in Dimapur,' say Gen. Muthanna. 'We felt a sense of immense sadness, for the loss of Mrs Rawat and for their orphaned daughters and the families of the others. We offered prayers for the recovery of the sole survivor, Group Captain Varun Singh and for his family. As military men, we are exposed to challenges and even face the possibility of death, but when families are killed the pain is even more intense. Prayers go out first for the families and then for the soldiers' souls,' he says.

# 'Unrest Was at Its Peak When He Came to Congo'

9 December 2021
New Delhi

Lt Gen. Jaiveer Singh Negi looked at the massive crowd that had started gathering around 3 Kamaraj Marg, where the mortal remains of General and Mrs Rawat were being kept. Television cameras were panning the area to show their viewers what a colossal sea of humanity had emerged on Delhi's streets to pay respects to the late Chief of Defence Staff.

Gen. and Mrs Negi had driven down from Dehradun to pay their last respects to the couple they had developed a deep admiration for over the years. They had been looking forward to meeting the Rawats in Dehradun, where they were to attend the Indian Military Academy's passing out parade. Instead, they were now in Delhi to attend their funeral.

A day earlier, Jaiveer had been travelling when he received the shocking news from a colleague that the helicopter taking Gen. Rawat to Wellington had crashed. By evening, it was announced that the General and Mrs Rawat had not survived.

The news had taken time to sink in. Some people were expressing surprise at how deeply even people who had never met Gen. Rawat were grief-stricken at his shocking demise. Jaiveer was not surprised at all. He knew how Bipin could endear himself to people, be it in India or abroad. He had seen that happening in Congo.

\* \* \*

August 2008
North Kivu
The Democratic Republic of Congo

Col Jaiveer Singh Negi was Deputy Commander of the United Nations' North Kivu Brigade in the Democratic Republic of the Congo (formerly known as Zaire), when then Brigadier Bipin Rawat came to Goma, the capital of North Kivu and—exchanging his Gorkha Rifles hat for a blue UN beret—took over as Commander of the Indian Army's largest deployment on foreign soil.

It was a very demanding time in the world's most challenging peacekeeping mission, known by its French acronym MONUC. 'Unrest was at its peak, rebel activities were rising, and there was a lot of apprehension about the performance of UN and Indian troops,' Gen. Jaiveer remembers. 'The National Army was not being able to control the rebels, law-and-order problems were increasing, and the local population was losing confidence in the UN force.'

Brig. Rawat was surprised to find that public opinion was against the Indian contingent, and there were frequent cases of mobbing and stone-pelting at UN vehicles on the streets of Goma, where part of the Indian brigade was based. The general feeling was that they were not doing enough for the local people and were not welcome in Congo.

'It was a difficult moment for a new Commander to step in,' explains Gen. Jaiveer. 'The challenge before him was not just planning and execution of operations, and the performance of his own troops. Since the UN had a combined and multinational force, he was also responsible for the troops of other countries that had been placed under the Indian brigade, and elements like attack helicopters of the army as well as air force. All operations were a combined exercise and needed teamwork. Since the UN force was mainly meant to be in a supporting role to the local government forces, the Indian brigade was also responsible for training the Congolese Army, called the FARDC [Forces armées de la république démocratique du Congo], and for motivating them, because they were the ones who had to fight the rebels.'

Bipin also had to work on gaining the confidence of the force headquarters, force commander and the mission head, the Special Representative of Security General (SRSG), etc., all of whom had been under pressure due to rising rebel activities.

It was a lot to ask for, but Bipin remained characteristically unfazed. He took on his new responsibilities with fortitude. He would sit through endless briefings to understand and assess the situation. He would go around to see the area for himself and with Jaiveer, sometimes travelling to the force headquarters in Kinshasha, the capital of the Democratic Republic of the Congo. He was sharp, a keen listener, and quick to grasp the situation and understand what needed to be done. Within a month he decided to turn the soft strategy the UN was following to a tough one.

'We have not been using our equipment to the optimum, despite Chapter Seven of the UN Charter authorizing the use of force in some scenarios. We have decided to operate with our full equipment, which includes armoured vehicles and attack helicopters,' he told media representatives covering the conflict, and soon put that into action by ordering the use of attack helicopters and armoured combat vehicles against rebels, shocking them completely. The protection of civilians, domination of areas, taking action against rebels involved in the recruitment of child soldiers and minimizing displacement of the population became his priority areas.

His professionalism, and the physical and moral courage he possessed were quickly passed down to his troops as he took some bold decisions and got them implemented.

'There was a fair amount of risk-taking involved,' recollects Gen. Jaiveer. 'But he knew his mind well as well as the capabilities of the Indian troops. While on the ground he was an astute commander, he could stand up and talk with complete conviction at meetings in the Force Headquarters and with UN agencies. He would respond firmly to any adverse comments about the Indian contingent and India.'

Bipin Rawat's residence in North Kivu was about 15 km away from where the troops were stationed. Since the prevailing situation made it difficult for him to travel the distance every day, he shifted to the troops' location. Two containers were modified, and he moved into one, spending nearly two months of conflict right in the midst of where the unrest was, living in a container adjacent to the one in which Jaiveer was putting up.

The biggest challenge in Congo was that it was impossible for the force to be present everywhere, because the area was vast and armed rebel groups could strike just anywhere or at multiple places at the same time. It was not possible to patrol and dominate the entire area at all times. Bipin, however, remained unfazed. Two major conflicts took place, and he handled both with clarity and level-headedness.

Gen. Jaiveer remembers how Brig. Rawat would formulate the plan and set guidelines, but 'he gave me and the units full freedom to function thereafter'. He cites an instance when armed groups took over large areas in North Kivu and started moving towards its capital, Goma.

'The situation had become critical since the government machinery and civilian administration collapsed completely,' he says. 'The mayor came and took shelter in one of our unit bases.' Assessing the deteriorating situation, and the criticality of protecting Goma and Masisi, Brig. Rawat decided to use attack helicopters. 'That was the first time we used gunships of our air force contingent, and were able to halt the advance of the rebels and push them out from the areas they had taken over,' Gen. Negi explains.

The multinational troops and Indian battalions supported by BMPs—Russian-made armoured vehicles fitted with machine guns—were also used against the rebels, who could not stand the former's might and finally withdrew. The advance of rebel forces was halted just 10 km short of Goma.

'If that hadn't been done, Goma would have fallen,' Gen. Negi says.

In a remarkable turnaround, the UN force that had been facing public anger till then became a beacon of hope and survival for the locals. The fall of Masisi, an important town in North Kivu province about 80 km from Goma, was prevented and a lot of civilian casualties avoided. Hundreds of locals, caught in the crossfire between the Congolese forces and rebel fighters, went to the UN base in Masisi and took asylum. They clapped and cheered when Indian helicopters strafed rebel positions with rockets, supporting the state forces as they fought and pushed the rebels back.

At one point, the rebel groups went and placed themselves in areas between North Kivu and South Kivu, severing the connection between the two provinces. While the Indian force was in North Kivu, it so happened that a Pakistani battalion was located in South Kivu. Since both countries were working under the UN umbrella, there was frequent interaction between them. When armed rebels managed to cut off the two areas, it created a very serious situation for the UN. The brigade had to launch an operation to dislodge the rebel groups.

'Brig. Rawat used to be present for all plans, aerial surveys and discussions,' says Gen. Jaiveer.

A massive military operation was planned, and after intense operations, the UN forces finally removed the wedge and pushed out the rebel groups between North and South Kivu, and communication and road contact was re-established.

Gen. Jaiveer remembers how the success of the operation was appreciated by all concerned. The SRSG, who headed the mission, came down to Goma, and since Bipin was away, Col. Jaiveer flew with him on a chopper, over the area from North Kivu to South Kivu, and explained to him how the operations were launched and rebels pushed out to restore the situation and link up the two places. The helicopter finally landed at the Pakistani battalion post in South Kivu, and the SRSG was convinced that rebels had been defeated and peace restored. The success of the operation restored the credibility and reputation of the Indian troops and the UN in a big way.

Later, UN Secretary General Ban Ki-moon flew to Kinshasha from the UN headquarters to hold talks with the Congolese government and assess the situation. He visited the Indian brigade in Goma and had a meal with the officers and soldiers. Speaking at the gathering, he expressed his admiration for India. While recounting the bravery of Capt. Gurbachan Singh Salaria—who had also been with the UN forces in Congo and attained martyrdom fighting the rebels in 1962—he said that Congo stood united because of the UN forces and specially mentioned India's contribution. A satisfied Brig. Rawat smiled quietly from where he was listening.

'It was a great professional achievement,' says Gen. Jaiveer. 'The brigade had performed very well. India's glory was restored.' In appreciation of the work done, Brig. Rawat was awarded the Force Commander's commendation while citations were awarded to the Indian units. Level-three military hospitals were established by India in Goma. Many officers and troops, including Col Jaiveer, were awarded the Force Commander's commendations.

The brigade continued to perform well thereafter, and as Brig. Rawat's one-year term came close to its end, the Force Commander implored him to stay back. Though he was a Brigadier, he was addressed as Brigadier General in the UN assignment. Gen. Jaiveer remembers the request when the Force Commander came and said, 'General Bipin, the force has performed so well under you that we would like you to stay on. If you don't mind, we are going to ask for an extended tenure for you.'

Brig. Rawat called up the army headquarters the very next day, reported the conversation and told them that a request might come from the UN to extend his tenure in Congo, but in no way should it be construed as coming from him. 'I am ready to go on my next assignment, wherever it may be,' he said. And, in fact, he did not stay another day after his tenure ended.

## Personal Qualities That Made Him Stand Apart

Gen. Jaiveer talks about Bipin Rawat's wholehearted participation in social events and family functions of his colleagues: 'Gen. and Mrs Rawat would make it a point to attend all the functions that they were invited to. I remember instances when, in spite of having just landed at the Delhi airport after a visit, they would quickly change in some guestroom and attend the function they had been invited for, even if their busy schedule allowed them only 15–20 minutes.'

He says they attended his son's wedding in Delhi Cantonment in 2018, where Gen Rawat made it a point to inquire where Jaiveer's parents were. When he found that Jaiveer's mother was wheelchair-bound, he went across to where the elderly couple were and congratulated them. 'These were the qualities that set him apart from other people,' says Gen. Jaiveer.

He also narrates an incident from 2005, when Bipin Rawat had taken a study leave after the end of his tenure at the Military Secretary's branch in Army HQ. About twenty days before his study leave was to end, he called up Jaiveer, who was then posted as Colonel MS, responsible for postings and study leaves of infantry officers.

'Since by that time Col Bipin had been approved for his next rank and would have got his posting in a few months, I expected him to tell me to keep him in Delhi on some attachment for a few months before his promotion and next move, to avoid double moves, but he told me to post him out. "Send me wherever you want to. When my posting comes, I shall go and join the new place. You don't have to keep me in Delhi in the interim period. Since I have served in MS Branch, I know what problems that can create and don't want to do it,"' Gen. Jaiveer recollects.

In conclusion, Gen. Jaiveer says, 'Both Gen. and Mrs Rawat were simple, down-to-earth people, who touched people's lives and hearts. It was obvious in the mass outpouring at their funeral that people from all walks of life were grief-stricken at their demise and felt an immense sense of loss.'

# A Man in a Hurry

8 December 2021
India International Centre
Delhi
2 p.m.

Retired Lt General Subrata Saha, former Deputy Chief of Army Staff, was at the India International Centre when he noticed a news notification on his cellphone. It mentioned that a helicopter carrying India's Chief of Defence Staff had crashed in Tamil Nadu. Shocked, he called up the CDS but could not get through. Eventually, he rang up a friend at HQ IDS (Integrated Defence Staff), only to be told that 'the news was not very good'.

Gen. Saha's heart sank. He had known Bipin from when they were seventeen-year-olds at the National Defence Academy. It had been an association of forty-seven years. Gen. Saha looked back sentimentally on the friendship that had grown as they had risen in service and as their hair had greyed with time.

\* \* \*

'My intuition was that Bipin was gone,' says Gen. Saha, speaking about the day he learnt of the terrible accident. 'Why so soon? I asked myself, praying fervently that my gut feeling was wrong.'

The two of them had been together from the fifty-third course at the NDA. Saha had retired as Deputy Chief of Army Staff in March 2017. Bipin was the Chief at that time. Gen. Saha says that one of his fondest memories of his very gracious friend pertains to his own dining-out, where Bipin was the chief host. The formal dinner was organized at the Battle Honours Mess on Sardar Patel Marg in New Delhi.

After the meal was over, Bipin stood up to make the farewell speech and to propose a toast to all the officers retiring that month. Standing upright in his Six Bravo—white half shirt sparkling with epaulettes, black trousers crisply ironed, regimental kamarbandh wrapped around his waist—he smiled and looked at Saha, and then told the gathering, 'I have to confess that I managed to pass my staff college only because Saha so generously shared his notes with me.' And then, displaying his typical sense of humour, he added, 'But let me tell you that Saha did not give me his number-one notes. I know this because he made it to Camberley in the United Kingdom, while I could only make it to Wellington.' 'The entire lot of officers and ladies gathered there broke into laughter,' Gen. Saha fondly remembers.

'Bipin and I passed out from NDA in December 1977, and passed out of IMA and got commissioned together on 16 December 1978,' he says. 'Bipin had been six months senior to us in NDA. He had joined in June 1974 but after his relegation, he came to our course in January 1975. From there we came to the Indian Military Academy, which was where he really started shining and getting noticed.'

Soon after they were commissioned, the two officers served together as Second Lieutenants in 9 Independent Mountain Brigade at Joshimath, though in different sectors. In 1987, they both got posted to the Indian Military Academy as instructors. 'We were

Captains at that time, and that was the time when we became really good friends,' remembers Gen. Saha. 'Bipin was a platoon commander with the Army Cadet College Wing, while I was a platoon commander in Bhagat Battalion's Keren Company.'

He remembers Bipin as a strict though compassionate platoon commander who cared for his cadets, as if they were his own children, but was also emphatic that they do well and pick up the qualities that were important for them to grow in service. Many years later, the two friends served as Chief and Deputy Chief of Army Staff together, from where Gen. Saha retired and Gen. Rawat went on to become Chief of Defence Staff.

'It was a coincidence that we kept getting posted to the same organizations throughout our careers,' says Gen. Saha. 'In 2001, I got posted to Army HQ, Delhi, as Col MS2 [Military Secretary 2, responsible for career management of infantry officers]. Exactly one year later, Bipin came in as Col MS3 [responsible for all NCC postings and deputations], and we would meet every single day at the morning conference of the Deputy MS.'

Serving in the MS branch was tough since the postings and promotions of officers had to be balanced with individual expectations and organizational requirements, but Bipin managed very well. 'He was pragmatic and compassionate at the same time. If a case was genuine and the intent good, Bipin could go to any extent to make sure that the requirement was met,' Gen. Saha remembers.

As Brigadiers, the two were together again in Kashmir in 2007–8. Bipin commanded 5 Sector Rashtriya Rifle in north Kashmir, while Saha commanded 268 Infantry Brigade on the Line of Control, undertaking counter-infiltration operations. 'We exchanged notes frequently,' recalls Gen. Saha, smiling as he remembers Bipin's characteristic wit. 'He would mostly call off by saying, "*Do chaar chhor de—yahaan bhi dhum-dhadaka ho* (Let go of some terrorists—let there be bang-bang here as well)."'

## A Soldier's General

In 2013–14, Bipin was serving as MGGS (Major General, General Staff), Operations, at Headquarters, Eastern Command, Calcutta, while Saha was serving as Additional Director, General Military Operations, in Delhi.

'Bipin's area of responsibility was huge—stretching all the way from Sikkim to Arunachal and including all areas along the India–China border and Myanmar,' he explains. 'As ADG MO, it was my responsibility to speak to the MGGS of Northern and Eastern Commands every morning to check if all had been okay in their areas in the past twenty-four hours. So in that period I spoke to him every day, come rain, hail, sunshine, holidays, Sundays. Sometimes, we would even do two to three calls in a day,' he says with a smile.

He remembers a day in August 2013 when he was in his office. Around 6 p.m., he noticed that one of the television sets in the room was playing a story about an altercation between Indian and Chinese troops, which had happened in Yangtse in the Eastern Sector. He quickly called up Bipin, asking him if he had seen the news. Bipin hadn't but said that it had been conveyed to him by someone.

'Of course, as it always is in the forces, the first concern was, "How did the video leak?"' Gen. Saha explains. 'But we also noticed how a small group of our soldiers was so boldly standing up to a much larger number of Chinese soldiers from the People's Liberation Army.'

Bipin quickly grasped the point and explained this to his boss, convincing him that the soldiers deserved a pat on the back. Soon after, troops who had been a part of that face-off were awarded commendation cards. The video leak was investigated as well.

'That was the kind of man Bipin was,' says Gen. Saha. 'He could quickly grasp and respond to a situation. He could stand up for his men, and he could remain unfazed under all circumstances.'

Gen. Saha remembers a call he made to his friend on the evening Bipin had survived a helicopter crash in Dimapur while serving as

GOC, 3 Corps. 'Bipin dismissed it with a casual "all my bones are intact" and laughed heartily.'

He can also vividly recall their conversations after the Myanmar attack, when Bipin was GOC, 3 Corps; after Uri, when Bipin was Vice Chief; and even after Doklam, when Bipin was Chief. These were all situations to which Bipin responded fiercely, stating that what had happened was unacceptable.

'He was absolutely unshaken and very clear in his resolve that we had to give it back, because if we didn't, it was bound to happen again. He was in full control of the situation at all times and ready to deal with it. He undertook some very good operations. Bipin was instrumental in the decisions that were taken,' Gen. Saha says.

He also points out that Bipin Rawat had the moral courage to take a stand where it was required and accept blame. 'He had the broad shoulders to accept responsibility. He was the kind of man people would readily accept as a commander, because they knew that in times of crisis *kuchh ho bhi gaya toh peechhe Commander hain, sambhal lenge* (whatever happened, Commander will handle it),' says Gen Saha.

Gen. Saha met a Subedar Major a day after the unfortunate helicopter crash. '*Sahab, jis din ye hua, hamari unit mein zyadatar logon ne khana nahi khaya* (On the day it happened, most people in my unit didn't eat),' he told Gen Saha, '*Jitna Rawat Sahab ne jawano ke liye koshish kiya, bahut kam logon ne kiya* (Few people did as much for the jawans as Rawat Sahab).'

Gen. Saha draws attention to the cadre review Bipin had introduced for JCOs and Other Ranks in December 2017, exactly a year after he took over as COAS. The number of vacancies for JCOs and NCOs increased because of this.

'Bipin was genuinely concerned about the welfare of troops. He knew that when more people are promoted the level of satisfaction increases,' Gen. Saha explains. 'The void that the JCOs and ORs felt was very significant. When he became the first CDS of the country, people had hopes from him. They believed in him and his desire to do something for them.'

## A Man for Modernization

Gen. Saha likes to point out how committed Bipin Rawat was to indigenization. 'In 2015, an intensive drive for indigenization, involving the industry and academia, had been started,' he says. 'This was happening under a drive I used to describe as "Win India's Wars with Indian Solutions".'

A team comprising Gen. Saha and six Brigadiers organized army–industry–academia engagements at various academic and industrial hubs, almost every weekend, from the end of 2015 to early 2017.

'The idea was to tell them what we need in the next fifteen years,' he explains. 'Bipin was immensely excited by the happenings soon after he became the Vice Chief. We signed MOUs with many IITs. We were able to post army officers to IIT Gandhinagar, IIT Mumbai and IIT Madras. In fact, Bipin made sure that the prime minister was briefed by me on this initiative at the Army House on the occasion of Army Day on 15 January 2017. Bipin sought modernization, not just in terms of weapons and technology, but also mindsets, right down to the troops level. An effort was made to inculcate technology into the syllabus at every level. If a soldier was doing a course on machine guns, an effort was made to teach him the latest technology in machine guns. Bipin looked at reforms in totality.'

## Hide of a Rhino

Gen. Saha says his last memories of his friend are of a man who had taken on a lot and was trying to do it all in the limited time he had. 'I was a member of the National Security Advisory Board, and once in a month we would sit in his office and exchange views on several things. Many times he would say, "Look, I am around till 31 December 2022, and I have to achieve this." He had embarked on so much, and not all the things he wanted to do were easy. He knew there were headwinds he would have to sail through. He did not fear criticism. He did not hesitate to say something just because somebody might not like it. He would say and do what he believed in. Not everyone can do that,' says Gen. Saha.

Gen. Saha would often joke that though he himself was from the Assam Regiment, it was Bipin who had the thick hide of a rhino, and Bipin would laugh heartily at that.

'He was aware of the kind of expectations people had from him—right from the highest leadership to the troops. He was trying to get things done. He never let any flak interfere with his decision-making. He was a sincere soldier. His intent was good,' says Gen. Saha.

## Bipin's Legacy

'His legacy is the national defence reforms. They have not been concluded yet, but they are halfway home. It is just as well that this is happening a little deliberately, since any reforms of that magnitude in the armed forces of the size that we have need to be brought in with care. The process is on, and it will get done. The first integrated command will be the greatest tribute to General Bipin Rawat,' concludes Gen. Saha.

# A Reluctant Colonel Commandant

Lt Gen. Rakesh Sharma and Gen. Bipin Rawat, who were Second Lieutenants in 5/11 GR together, went on to become best friends. They also had interlinked careers. 'When I commanded 5/11, Bipin was my 2IC,' says Gen. Sharma with a smile. 'Years later, when he became Vice Chief, I was serving as the Adjutant General, Indian Army. And he also took over as Colonel of the Regiment (COR) from me.' (The Colonel of the Regiment is usually the senior-most officer of the regiment, who is a father figure to all serving men and looks after their interests. He represents the regiment at the higher level of military hierarchy.)

Gen. Sharma seldom talks about the fact that he voluntarily resigned as COR nearly a year before his retirement because he wanted Bipin to take over. And that it took him nearly eight months to convince Bipin to become the Colonel. It is only after much prodding that he shares that interesting story.

# The Reluctant Colonel of the Regiment

In September 2015, Bipin was commanding 3 Corps in Dimapur and Rakesh was Adjutant General, Indian Army. It was known that Bipin would take over as Army Commander on 1 December. On a Delhi trip, Bipin came over for lunch to Rakesh's South Block office, as he always did whenever the two friends happened to be free. After a fond embrace, Rakesh looked at the old friend smiling at him from across the table and said, 'Bipin, you going to become Army Commander. I feel you should now take over as Colonel of the Regiment.'

Bipin watched him with narrowed eyes. '*Nahi*, sir,' he replied emphatically. 'I shall take over only after you retire. *Jab tak aap hain* (As long as you are around), you are the Colonel.'

Rakesh had a year and a half to go for retirement. He tried to reason with Bipin, but the latter absolutely refused to listen. Lunch over, the two friends parted.

In December, Bipin became Army Commander and was initially posted as General Officer Commanding, Maharashtra, Gujarat and Goa Area, for a month—the appointment that his father had also held many years back, with Rakesh as the senior Gen. Rawat's ADC.

'My wife, daughter and I went to Mumbai to congratulate Bipin and stayed with the Rawats in Gun House [the GOC's residence] in Colaba. It was a nostalgic trip,' remembers Gen. Sharma.

That was the second time he broached the subject of COR with his friend. 'You have become Army Commander. You should now take over as Colonel of the Regiment,' he told Bipin, highlighting to him that their Regiment (11 GR) was making an Army Commander after a very long time. (The last Army Commander had been Gen. Rocky Hira in late 1970s, also in the Southern Command.)

'I told him it was a matter of great pride and privilege for the regiment and that he should take over as Colonel,' Gen. Sharma recollects. But Bipin was his usual stubborn self and refused to entertain the idea.

Rakesh went back to Delhi and discussed his desire with then Army Chief Gen. Dalbir Suhag, who was also from the Gorkha Rifles and President of the Gorkha Brigade. A month later, Bipin took over as Southern Army Commander in Pune. Rakesh, who happened to go there on an official trip, stayed with him and again broached the subject, which Bipin again refused to listen to.

'It took me nearly eight months to convince Bipin and the Chief, and finally, in April 2016, Bipin agreed to take over as Colonel of the Regiment,' he says.

In June 2016, Rakesh went to the COAS and submitted his resignation as Colonel of the Regiment, and subsequently a formal ceremony was held at Manekshaw Centre, Delhi, where Gen. Bipin Rawat took over as Colonel of the Regiment. He gave a very touching speech, saying that even though he was now Colonel Commandant, he would still want Gen. Rakesh Sharma to remain at the helm of affairs. The old-timers from the regiment still remember the speech very fondly.

That was a time when it couldn't even be imagined that Bipin would go on to become Vice Chief or Chief. It was only on 1 September 2016 that he became Vice Chief. Gen. Sharma continued to serve as Adjutant General.

On one occasion, the COAS, Gen. Dalbir Suhag, was flanked by Lt Gen. Bipin Rawat, VCOAS, on one side and Lt Gen. Rakesh Sharma, AG, on the other. That was when Gen. Rakesh quipped to the Chief saying how lucky he was, flanked by two Generals, both from 5/11 GR.

Gen. Sharma retired from service in March 2017 and was dined out by Bipin, who had by then become COAS. Giving the farewell speech, Bipin spoke movingly about the lifelong bond of friendship the four of them—Bipin, Rakesh, Payal and Madhu—shared.

# Not a Man to Take Things Lying Down

## The Myanmar Surgical Strike

4 June 2015
Chandel district
Manipur
9 a.m.

A military convoy of 6 Dogra is on its daily road opening patrol (ROP) about 80 km from Imphal. It is between Paralong and Charong villages in Chandel district when a powerful explosion takes place. One of the trucks is blown up by a powerful IED. The shocked and wounded soldiers scampering out of their vehicles are attacked by insurgents heavily armed with RPGs and automatic guns. Twenty soldiers are killed and eleven seriously injured in the brutal attack.

Lt Gen. Bipin Rawat is General Officer Commanding (GOC) of the Dimapur-based 3 Corps. Retaliation from the Indian Army is almost instantaneous. On 9 June, Para Commandos cross into

Myanmar and attack two camps of the NSCN-K and the NSCN-IM, militant organizations believed to be responsible for the attack on the Indian Army convoy. They reportedly kill 15–20 terrorists.

\* \* \*

'The decision to strike back was taken at the highest level. Bipin devised a plan, collected a team, came to Delhi, got the plan approved and put it into action,' remembers Gen. Rakesh Sharma. 'He was not a man to take things lying down.'

As per the details shared later, a crack team of around seventy commandos from 21 Para was chosen for the attack. Dhruv helicopters were used to drop them on the Myanmar border. Armed with rocket launchers, assault rifles and grenades, and wearing night vision glasses and uniforms of 12 Bihar, which happened to be the unit deployed at the border, the commandos were split into two teams. Each team took on one pre-identified camp. Each of the two teams further divided into two sub-groups and moved in two circles. While one carried out the main assault, the second formed an outer ring to prevent survivors from the camp from escaping.

The commandos entered the thick forest and walked about five kilometres to reach the training camps. They wrapped up the operation in forty minutes, destroying the camps, killing nearly thirty-eight Naga insurgents and injuring many others. Rocket launchers were used and gunfights were carried out in the operation, which ended with one of the camps being set on fire. Though Mi-17 helicopters were kept ready on the Indian side, as an emergency measure in case the commandos needed quick evacuation, the operation went through perfectly. It was overseen by Gen. Rawat and coordinated by Gen. Dalbir Singh Suhag, then Chief of Army Staff.

The operation became controversial when the information minister, Rajyavardhan Singh Rathore lauded the operation and declared that the Indian troops had crossed the Myanmar border. The Myanmar government denied that the operation had taken place on its territory. Zaw Htay, director in the Myanmar President's office, made this statement to the media: 'We will not allow any foreign military operations in Myanmar territory. Every country must respect the other country's sovereignty.' Possibly fearing a diplomatic flare-up, the Indian government immediately stopped any more official reports after that.

However, two years later, in December 2017, Gen. Rawat spoke openly about the operation at a book release function in Pune, admitting that it was a cross-border raid carried out by the Indian Army on NSCN-K militant hideouts in Myanmar. He said Special Force commandos had faced many difficulties in Myanmar 'after crossing over' but the militant camp on the other side recorded 'heavy losses'.

Rawat even told the Pune gathering that he had to alter the original plan because of a call from National Security Adviser Ajit Doval, who asked for the commando team leader to be recalled and briefed before launching the operation. Rawat said that he was taken aback by this, because the mission had already been launched. 'The troops which had reached the Myanmar border had to later change their route while carrying out the operation, four days from the day it was initially planned,' he said, confirming that the commandos had put on the uniforms of 12 Bihar, the unit deployed on the border, to facilitate the attack.

This was the first time anyone had spoken about the operations so openly, and there was a furore over his statements, with many calling it a diplomatic gaffe, particularly his assertion that more such surgical strikes could be undertaken 'if required'.

'Bipin was not a diplomat,' says Gen. Sharma, analysing the decisions taken by Gen. Bipin Rawat. 'He would always state his point with vehemence, whether the other party liked it or not. Hiding behind the veil of diplomacy was not his style. He always spoke his mind.'

As he had done about Myanmar, Bipin spoke his mind about Balakot too.

* * *

18 September 2016
12 Brigade Headquarters
Uri

It was a beautiful Sunday morning in Uri, a small town nestled in the lap of the Pir Panjal range, with the Jhelum River flowing nearby. In the army cantonment that housed the 12 Brigade Headquarters, there was some activity going on since a handing-taking-over process between two units was on. While one unit had completed its two-year tenure and was moving out, the other was moving in.

Some of the soldiers from the incoming unit were sleeping in tents put up for them near the administrative block, while others were refilling 200-litre diesel barrels at the fuel depot that stocked diesel, petrol and kerosene meant for army vehicles and for cooking food in high-altitude posts.

The soldiers were completely oblivious to the fact that four armed *fidayeen* (terrorists on a suicidal mission) had entered the premises. The four of them had crossed the border and walked six kilometres to reach the camp. Taking cover behind the tall grass growing around the campus, they had managed to reach the administrative block undetected. All four were heavily armed. Not only were they carrying AK-47 rifles with grenade launchers clipped under their barrels, they had also brought more than fifty incendiary grenades, especially designed to set off fires. As soon as they spotted the fuel dump, the militants lobbed as many as seventeen grenades, setting the dump on fire and taking the soldiers there completely by surprise.

The ammunition dump exploded, and amid the screams of injured soldiers and the crackle of flames leaping high into the sky, the militants ran into the nearby barracks. The fire spread quickly to the tents, enveloping all that fell in its path in massive flames. Thirteen unsuspecting soldiers, still asleep, were burnt to death almost instantaneously; some succumbed to their burns later in the hospital.

One of the terrorists was shot down by an alert soldier, while the others ran deeper into the building. Their original plan had been to find their way to the officers' mess and blow themselves up there, but the fumes and smog had disoriented the fidayeen. Taking cover in the second floor of the building, they started firing. After a six-hour-long gunfight, the three militants were killed. They were later identified as belonging to the militant outfit Jaish-e-Mohammed.

While unrest in Kashmir had been increasing since 2015, Uri's was the biggest terrorist attack on an army camp in twenty-six years. Eighteen soldiers lost their lives and more than thirty were wounded. The incident shocked the entire country, causing a huge public outcry.

On 1 September 2016, Bipin had been brought to Delhi and made Vice Chief of Army Staff after a short eight-month tenure as General Officer Commanding-in-Chief (GOC-in-C), Southern Command, in Pune.

'Uri jolted people out of their seats. There had been sporadic incidents of violence earlier too, but this time everyone was badly shaken. Bipin was furious,' remembers Lt Gen. Rakesh Sharma, who was serving as Adjutant General of the Indian Army when Lt Gen. Rawat took over as Vice Chief. The two friends, who had started their careers together in 5/11 GR as young officers, were together once again, this time in two of the Indian Army's highest appointments. And both were equally upset by what had happened.

'Bipin made his views clear. "We cannot take this quietly. We have to do something," he said vociferously, in private as well as while addressing the parliamentary committee, which was at that time headed by Maj. Gen. B.C. Khanduri,' says Gen. Sharma.

This was a sentiment echoed by the higher-ups as well. A cross-border retaliatory strike was cleared by Prime Minister Narendra Modi. Then Defence Minister Manohar Parrikar, National Security Adviser Ajit Doval, then Army Chief Gen. Dalbir Singh Suhag and then Northern Army Commander Lt Gen. D.S. Hooda had a major role to play in its planning and implementation. 'Though the decision was taken at the highest level, Bipin definitely had a role to play in it. He was not a man who would take things lying down. He had always been like that,' says Gen. Sharma.

## 'We Had to Respond'

Just ten days after the Uri attack, India carried out stringent surgical strikes in Pakistan Occupied Kashmir. Two teams of commandos from the elite 2 Para crossed the border and attacked two terrorism centres, inflicting heavy casualties on the militants. After the strikes, the DGMO made a public declaration that Pakistan had been informed, and though the Indian Army would not continue the engagement, it was ready for any kind of reaction from its neighbour.

After the successful surgical strike, both Bipin and Gen. Sharma drove down to Parliament House Annexe together. Gen. Sharma says, 'The Military Operations Directorate used to come under the Vice Chief at that time, so Bipin was directly involved. Both of us had briefings, and we sat outside the conference room together. Bipin was emphatic that there was no question of not responding. "We could not have taken this lying down. We had to respond," he had stated, firmly and clearly.'

## Tenure as Chief of Army Staff

On 17 December 2016, the Government of India appointed Bipin Rawat as the twenty-seventh Chief of the Army Staff. The appointment created a lot of controversy since he had superseded two senior officers—Lt Gen. Praveen Bakshi and Lt Gen. P.M. Hariz. He took over on 31 December 2016, after Gen. Dalbir Singh

Suhag retired. He was the third officer from the Gorkhas to become COAS, the first two being Field Marshal Sam Manekshaw and the second Gen. D.S. Suhag.

## The Balakot Strike

On 14 February 2019, around 3.15 p.m., a convoy of seventy-eight vehicles bringing Central Reserve Police Force (CRPF) jawans from Jammu to Srinagar was attacked by a terrorist who drove an explosive-laden car into one of the buses, leading to the death of forty CRPF personnel and the perpetrator. The attack took place on the Jammu–Srinagar national highway at Lethpora in Pulwama district of J&K. The suicide bomber was later identified as twenty-year-old Adil Ahmed Dar. The Pakistan-based Islamist militant group Jaish-e-Mohammed took responsibility for the killings, though Pakistan condemned the attack and denied any involvement. The entire nation was stunned by this cold-blooded killing of unarmed troops.

On 26 February, at around 3.30 a.m., in a retaliatory attack, Indian Air Force planes struck a Jaish-e-Mohammed facility in Balakot (Khyber Pakhtunkhwa). India stated that the mission had eliminated 'a large number of terrorists, their handlers and supporters', and that the IAF planes had returned home unharmed. The strikes were described as 'non-military' and 'pre-emptive' in nature. The Prime Minister, the National Security Adviser, the chiefs of the three services and heads of India's external and internal intelligence agencies (RAW and IB) were the only people who knew about the entire operation. And it was declared that it had been a success. Pakistan, however, announced that the Indian aircraft were intercepted soon after they entered Pakistan's airspace and were forced to retreat, after releasing their bombs in an open area.

WikiLeaks, quoting a 2004 United States Department of Defence interrogation report, confirmed that Balakot had 'a training camp offering basic as well as advanced terrorist training on explosives and artillery', but Western security officials doubted India's claims and insisted that no large-scale militant camps existed in Pakistan any more, though this was the first time that warplanes had crossed the Line of Control since the India–Pakistan war of 1971.

Ambiguity remained over the attacks till September that year, when Gen. Bipin Rawat once again spoke to the media openly, this time about Balakot. Talking to the press at the inauguration of a Young Leaders Training Wing at the Officers Training Academy in Chennai, he said that the terrorist camp at Balakot, across the border in Pakistan, which was destroyed by the Indian armed forces through a surgical strike earlier that year had been 'reactivated' and 'at least 500 persons were waiting to infiltrate into India', though 'adequate measures have been taken to curb infiltration'.

He emphasized that the Indian Air Force must have destroyed something if it needed to be reactivated. On being asked if a repeat of India's response to Balakot could be expected, Gen. Rawat said, 'Why must we expect a repeat of a similar thing? Earlier we did something, then we did Balakot. Why not keep the other side guessing? Why tell them what we are going to do?'

This created a huge outcry in the country, with critics accusing him of being brash, but he did not retract any of his statements.

'Bipin was not a diplomat, he was a soldier,' says Gen. Sharma, standing by his comrade stoutly. 'He spoke his mind, and he stood by what he did or said. I admire him for it. He never let criticism faze him, and that was one of his greatest qualities.'

Gen. Sharma recalls something Bipin would often say: 'Sitting quietly is not a solution, some deterrence has to be created.' Gen. Sharma adds, 'He did what he believed in. Whether a long-term deterrence has been created or not, only time will tell.'

## Bipin Becomes India's First CDS

Gen. Bipin Rawat was appointed India's first Chief of Defence Staff on 31 December 2019, having served for three years as the Chief of Army Staff. He continued to express his views and do what he believed in, facing a lot of criticism for being brash and reckless.

Many proposals put forth during his term—like placing restrictions on CSD purchases, making defence area thoroughfares, integration of theatre commands—led to a strong backlash from serving as well as retired officers. He, however, remained characteristically unperturbed by criticism and was likened to a bull in a china shop by detractors who, though grudgingly, agreed that this kind of bull-headedness was often required to push people and get work done.

'Bipin was a fighter,' says Gen. Rakesh Sharma, defending the decisions Gen. Rawat took. 'He also had broad shoulders. Not only could he take bold decisions, he could also accept responsibility and criticism for those decisions. He would stand by what he said or did. For me, that made him a man of great courage and integrity.'

Bipin Rawat was known for giving the media headlines. But it is true that some of the boldest decisions taken by the armed forces happened during his time, and he seemed to have a significant role to play in their implementation. During his time, there was a marked shift in India's readiness to defend itself and, if necessary, to retaliate; its passive engagement policy on the Line of Control had become a thing of the past. India had not just carried out surgical strikes across the Line of Control in retaliation against acts of terrorism but had also admitted it publicly. Pakistan Army Chief Qamar Javed Bajwa later said that Balakot had changed Pakistan's threat perception from India. For the first time, India looked aggressive in combating cross-border terror sponsored by Pakistan.

*In this chapter, the Manipur attack of 4 June 2015 and its aftermath have been reconstructed from reports that appeared in* The Hindu. *Details of the Uri attack have been taken from an* India Today *report. Details of the retaliation to the Uri and Pulwama attacks have been taken from* Economic Times *reports. Gen. Bipin Rawat's quotes on the Balakot strike are from reports that appeared in* The Hindu.

# A General Who Stood by His Men

Gen. Bipin Rawat remained mired in controversy for his bold statements and stands taken, for which he received strong criticism throughout his tenure as COAS and CDS. Those who knew him well say that he was never diplomatic, which was due to his strength of character. Knowing brickbats would be hurled at him, he still stood by what he believed in.

'As Army Chief my concern is morale of the army. That is my job. I am far away from the battlefield. I cannot influence the situation there. I can only tell the boys that I am with you. I always tell my people, things will go wrong, but if things have gone wrong and you did not have malafide intent, I am there,' he told the Press Trust of India in an interview and proved that they weren't empty words.

In 2017, as Chief of Army Staff, he shocked his detractors and won the hearts of serving men in uniform by publicly standing by an officer who had been accused of human rights violation in Kashmir. Major Leetul Gogoi, accused of using a Kashmiri youth as human shield to protect his men from stone pelting by an unruly mob, was

awarded a Chief of Army Staff Commendation Card by General
Bipin Rawat for 'sustained efforts' in 'counterinsurgency operations'
barely a month after the incident, which had led to shock and anger
in the Kashmir Valley, a huge outcry from human rights activists
and calls for the officer to be punished.

## The Gogoi Story

On 14 April 2017, a nineteen-second video of a Kashmiri man in a
phiran tied to the front of an army jeep started circulating on Twitter.
An announcement could also be heard on the video. Someone was
using a public address system to say, '*Patharbaazon ka yeh haal hoga*
(This is how stone pelters shall be treated).' The incident evoked
outrage among people in the Valley, human rights activists and
political leaders, and led to a deepening of the rift between the army
and the civil population. Former chief minister Omar Abdullah,
shared the video, demanding immediate inquiry.

Investigations revealed that the video was taken on 9 April 2017
in Badgam, during the Srinagar Lok Sabha by-election. The local
man was identified as Farooq Ahmed Dar, a resident of Sitaharaan
village in Khag tehsil of Budgam, while the army unit involved was
53 Rashtriya Rifles. Dar told investigators that he had gone to cast
his vote and was on his way to his sister's house, where a bereavement
had taken place, when he was caught by the army. The unit's stand
was that he had been leading the stone pelters

On 23 May, Major Leetul Gogoi, from 53 Rashtriya Rifles, faced
the media. He took responsibility for the action that was making
newspaper headlines and narrated the entire incident in detail,
explaining what had transpired on 9 April. He said that around 9.15
a.m., he had received a call from an Indo–Tibetan Border Police
(ITBP) official in charge of the polling stations in Gundi Pora and
Utligam villages in Budgam, who told him that hundreds of people
had surrounded the polling stations, and were pelting stones at the
polling staff and the ITBP personnel on duty. 'I took my quick

reaction team (QRT) and reached Gundi Pora in thirty minutes,' Gogoi said. 'We managed to disperse the mob, and I myself went in with four men to ensure that those manning the booth were safe.'

At 10.30 a.m., while he was still in Gundi Pora, he received another distress call from the same ITBP officer, who said that a mob of 1200 had collected around the Utligam polling station, 1.5 km away, and was trying to set the polling booth on fire by pelting petrol bombs at it. Gogoi said he reached the spot with his QRT but could not even step out of his vehicle, because the crowd, which included women and children, started throwing stones at them. Despite repeated announcements on the megaphone, requesting the mob to give way and explaining that the army was there only to rescue the polling staff, the crowd continued the stone pelting.

Major Gogoi said that he spotted a short person standing close by who appeared to be instigating the stone throwers and asked his men to catch him. Evading the flying stones, he and his soldiers managed to catch the man who was trying to flee on his bike. Holding him captive, they then walked to the polling booth, his presence having stopped the stone pelting. They rescued four polling staff, seven ITBP personnel and one J&K Police constable. On the way back, their mine-protected vehicle got stuck in the mud, which gave the crowd another chance to start the stone pelting again.

'They became more violent, and a petrol bomb was also hurled, which, luckily, did not blast,' Maj. Gogoi told the media. He said when the crowd did not respond to his repeated requests to allow his men a safe passage so they could leave the area, the idea of tying up their captive on top of the vehicle came to him. It immediately stopped the stone pelting. 'We got a window to come out safely from that area,' Gogoi said, explaining that his move had saved lives of the civilian population.

'I did this only to save the local people. Had I fired, there would have been more than twelve casualties. With this idea I saved many people's lives,' he told reporters.

The action was criticized by human rights activists, who stated that forcing non-combatants to serve as human shields is a war crime according to the 1949 Geneva Conventions. Senior retired officers, like Lt Gen. H.S. Panag, felt that Gogoi had violated the Indian Army's ethos, standard operating procedures and rules of engagement. However, Gen. Rawat went ahead and awarded the COAS commendation to Maj. Gogoi for sustained efforts in counterinsurgency operations. He came in for a lot of criticism but characteristically stood by his decision.

Giving an interview to the Press Trust of India, Gen. Rawat said that the main objective of awarding Major Leetul Gogoi was to boost the morale of young officers who were operating in the militancy-infested state. 'The rules of engagements are there when the adversary comes face to face and fights with you. This is a proxy war, and proxy war is a dirty war. That is where innovation comes in. You fight a dirty war with innovations,' he said, in his characteristically blunt manner.

'People are throwing stones at us, people are throwing petrol bombs at us. If my men ask me, 'What do we do?' should I say, just wait and die? I will come with a nice coffin with a national flag, and I will send your bodies home with honour. Is it what I am supposed to tell them as chief? I have to maintain the morale of my troops who are operating there.'

While emphasizing that maximum restraint was being exercised in handling the situation in the Valley, he said that if in a country people lose their fear of the army, then the country is doomed. 'We are a friendly army, but when we are called to restore law and order, people have to be afraid of us,' he stated, drawing further criticism.

Gen. Rakesh Sharma says he can understand what went on in Bipin's mind. 'He had done a tenure in Uri and commanded the Rashtriya Rifles sector in Sopore. He had been in insurgency and suffered. He understood Maj. Gogoi's predicament.'

As a Brigade Commander, Rawat had commanded 5 Section of Rashtriya Rifles in Sopore, which, at that time, was a hotbed of militancy. He moved to Congo to head the multinational United Nations Peacekeeping Force thereafter and returned to Uri as General Officer Commanding (GOC), 19th Infantry Division after being promoted to the rank of Major General.

'He had considerable Kashmir experience and knew the ground reality,' says Gen. Sharma. 'What could Maj. Gogoi have done? Those people [the polling booth team] would have been killed if he had not taken this stand. Gogoi was the man on the spot. He knew what was best in those circumstances. That was Bipin's stand, and it made perfect sense,' says Gen. Sharma.

He adds that being Chief of Army Staff, Bipin Rawat could have easily soft-pedalled the issue and taken a more diplomatic path, but he did not do that. 'He chose to stand by his man. That just shows his character.'

## In Trouble, Once Again

On 23 May 2018, barely a year after the human-shield episode, Major Gogoi landed in the eye of a storm once again. He was caught posing as an Assamese businessman while checking into the Grand Mamta hotel in Srinagar with an eighteen-year-old Kashmiri girl. The hotel staff refused entry to the girl, quoting rules, which led to an altercation with Major Gogoi and his driver. Gogoi, his driver and the girl were detained for questioning at the Khanyar police station. Though the girl deposed before a magistrate, saying she had willingly gone out with Major Gogoi, who happened to be her Facebook friend, the 'national hero' from just a year earlier was found guilty by the army of an act 'in violation of good order and military discipline'. It included 'fraternising' with a local girl and 'being away from his place of duty in an operational area'.

Just a few days after Maj. Gogoi was caught, Gen. Rawat stated that if Maj. Gogoi had done anything wrong, he would be punished in such a way that it would serve as an example to others. '*Agar Major Gogoi ne koi galat karwahi kari hai, toh main aapko yaqeen ke sath keh sakta hoon, ki jaldi se jaldi usko saza di jayegi, aur saza aisi doonga main, ki woh ek udharan ban kar reh jayega,'* he had said.

Major Gogoi was punished. He had to lose six months in seniority and was moved out of Jammu and Kashmir. 'When Maj. Gogoi overstepped his limits and was found guilty of a transgression, Bipin did not hesitate to punish him. That shows honesty and character once again,' Gen. Sharma emphasizes.

One of the most criticized statements made by Gen. Rawat was about stone pelters in the Valley. 'I wish these people, instead of throwing stones at us, were firing weapons at us. Then I would have been happy. Then I could do what I wanted to do,' he had said.

Gen. Sharma feels Gen. Rawat did not always have these views. He shares a memory of Bipin when he was Brigade Commander at Sopore. 'I was in Udhampur in 2007 and had flown down to Srinagar. Bipin came to pick me up and took me to Sopore. He was very keen that I should listen to a briefing by one of the Commanding Officers. "You must listen to him, sir," he said. "He has not fired a single shot, but the whole city is under control. He has achieved it only through relationship building." Bipin was emphatic that this was how insurgency ought to be handled. He was very impressed by the fact that that young Colonel had managed peace without using force. When the character of terrorism in the Valley changed with stone throwing and terror activities going on in parallel, Bipin voiced his concerns and advocated strong measures,' he says.

*Details of Major Leetul Gogoi's story have been drawn from various media reports and an Aaj Tak interview with the officer.*

# When a Soldier Asked the Army Chief to Prove His Identity

November 2017
Vikram Vihar
New Delhi
8 p.m.

On a balmy winter evening, the doorbell rings in Brigadier Shivender's Vikram Vihar flat in Delhi. He and his wife have retired for the day and are watching television in their bedroom. They hear the Garhwali *bhulla* (sahayak) with them go to open the door, some conversation, and the sound of people coming in and sitting down. The boy comes in to inform the couple, '*Koi sahab aaye hain* (Some sahab is here),' and then leaves for the day.

Shivender puts on his slippers and walks out wondering who has come to call on him at that late hour without prior intimation. He is stunned to find a widely grinning General Bipin Rawat sprawling comfortably on his sitting-room sofa, casually dressed in trousers and a buttoned shirt. Madhulika is wearing a salwar kameez in her favourite yellow colour and looking at some pictures on the mantlepiece. She turns when she hears him coming and starts laughing at the surprised look on his face.

'I was shocked to find Bunny sitting there. He was the Chief of Army Staff at that time. There was a lot of protocol and security involved in his movement, and yet he had come to my house unescorted,' Brig. Shivender remembers. 'When I asked him, "Aap kaise aa gaye (How did you get here)?" he replied, "*Tujhse milne ka mann ho raha tha, isliye gaadi nikaali aur aa gaya* (I felt like meeting you, so I took out the car and came here)." He had driven down to Vikram Vihar from Army House, his official residence in the Taurus campus, in his Swift Dzire, without bringing any of his bodyguards or escort vehicles, and he was looking very pleased about it.'

The cousins sit and have a few drinks together, chat about family and friends, and, after having whatever was cooked in the house for dinner, Bipin and Madhulika leave. Bidding Shivender and Renu goodnight, they get in their car and drive back home.

During the course of the evening, Bipin narrates to Shivender how, on his way there, he was stopped at the Shankar Vihar entrance barricade near the United Services Institute by an alert sentry on duty who politely but firmly asked him who he was. 'I told him I was the Army Chief, at which the soldier wasn't impressed at all, and asked me to prove my identity,' Bipin says, laughing loudly.

The Army Chief was carrying his ID card, and immediately took it out and showed it to the young soldier, who inspected it closely and, once satisfied that the man wanting to drive into the cantonment was indeed an army officer, wished him, 'Jai Hind, sahab,' and allowed him in. 'He even saw my name but did not register that I was the Chief of Army Staff,' Bipin tells his hosts, a smile playing upon his face. He was quite pleased with the fact that a soldier was doing his duty so sincerely and totally unconcerned that he had not recognized his Chief.

'That was the kind of man he was,' says Brig. Shivender. 'Simple and sincere, with absolutely no ego about the appointment he held.'

## A Man of Principles

Gen. Bipin Rawat was a sentimental man, but his commitment to Olive Green always came before anything else, including his own family. Brig. Shivender calls his brother 'a tough husband but a man of principles'. He remembers an episode from Bipin's tenure as 3 Corps Commander, when Madhulika Rawat had to attend a family wedding in Dehradun, and he couldn't go with her. 'She was travelling alone, and called me up to ask if I would be able to book a guestroom for her and organize a vehicle that would pick her up from the railway station since she was taking the Shatabdi from Delhi to Dehradun,' Brig. Shivender remembers.

He authorized a guestroom and told her that it would be no problem at all. He then contacted the Deputy General Officer Commanding, 14 Division, Brig. Paritosh Pant. The room was booked and a vehicle detailed for Madhulika. A few days later, Shivender received a frantic call from Madhulika asking him to cancel the arrangements. 'She told me Bipin had somehow come to know about a room and vehicle being organized for her Dehradun trip. Bipin was furious and had told her to get it cancelled right away. He did not want any favours to be taken from the army.' The arrangements had to be cancelled, and Madhulika eventually stayed with some relatives and took an autorickshaw from the railway station, even though she was the Corps Commander's wife.

Brig. Shivender says Bipin was exactly the same with other people too. He had no patience with anyone looking for freebies. 'No one could ask him for any favours because he would curtly refuse. "*Tum businessman ho. Tum fauj mein kyun rehna chahte ho? Tum bahar jaake ruko* (You are a businessman. Why do you want to stay at an army facility? Stay somewhere else), these facilities are not for you," he once scolded a relative who wanted a room in an army mess,' Brig. Shivender says with a laugh, disclosing how people in the family often came to him for favours, saying they wouldn't go to Bipin, because '*wo toh sunega nahi* (he wouldn't listen)'.

Another unpopular move Gen. Bipin Rawat had made was to decrease the amount of liquor authorized to army officers from the canteen on subsidized rates. An army officer was authorized to buy ten bottles of liquor from the canteen at subsidized rates. In May 2018, a directive from Army Headquarters specified that out of this monthly quota an officer would now be allowed to buy only five bottles of liquor costing more than Rs 1000.

When Shivender brought this up in a casual conversation, Bipin asked him which officer could drink ten bottles of single malt in a month. 'He would sit there in front of me calculating on his fingertips,' says Brig. Shivender. 'One bottle has twelve pegs. Taking ten bottles home in a month *ka matlab hai tum chaar peg roz pee rahe ho, iska matlab hai tum ek sharabi ho* (would mean you are having four pegs a day, which further means you're an alcoholic),' he would say, adding in disgust, "*Aisa aadmi kaam kya karega* (How can such a man do any work)?" And Shivender would quietly stifle a smile.

'Bunny was always outspoken, and very clear about what he liked and what he did not like,' he says, remembering yet another episode from Bipin's tenure at the Indian Military Academy. 'He was a young Major then and would not go to play golf, because he never liked it and called it a public-relations exercise. One day, the IMA Commandant asked him, "Why don't you play golf, Bipin?" to which the young Major responded, "Sir, I find it a waste of time."'

# 'Impress Me with Work, Not Gifts'

8 December 2021
Mhow

Gen. Manoj Mukund Naravane, PVSM, AVSM, SM, VSM, Chief of Army Staff, had just finished the Infantry Commanders' Conference and was on his way to the helipad, from where a chopper would be flying him to Indore and then back to Delhi. The conference had gone well, and he was leaning back in the seat of the staff car, his mind relaxed, when he heard his cellphone ringing.

It was his Military Attaché calling. He gave Naravane the shocking news that the Mi-17 flying Chief of Defence Staff Gen. Bipin Rawat to Wellington had crashed. Though stunned, Gen. Naravane was not unduly perturbed. He knew the CDS as a tough soldier and, since no further information was available, felt confident that Gen. Rawat would come out of this unharmed, just as he had in an earlier helicopter hard-landing that had happened in Dimapur seven years back.

## Meeting Gen. Naravane

25 August 2022
20 Mandir Marg
New Delhi

A Sikh soldier steps forward to open the door of 20 Mandir Marg, a sprawling, tree-shaded bungalow in Delhi Cantonment, the present residence of General Manoj Mukund Naravane, twenty-eighth Chief of the Army Staff. The General, who retired on 30 April 2022, walks into the room in a white shirt and trousers. He is slim, stands ramrod straight and has sharp intelligent eyes that light up with a smile of recognition.

He speaks of the late Gen. Bipin Rawat with a lot of respect and affection, though he admits that they did have a difference of opinion sometimes. 'That is bound to happen with anyone that you work closely with,' he says candidly. And the fact is that the two Generals were together for nearly nine years, ever since 2013, when Gen. Rawat got posted in Calcutta as Major General General Staff (MGGS), Eastern Command, while then Maj. Gen. Naravane was serving as Inspector General of Assam Rifles (IGAR), at Kohima in Nagaland.

Thereafter, the two served together when Gen. Rawat was posted as Corps Commander, 3 Corps, headquartered in Dimapur; then when General Rawat became the Vice Chief and Gen. Naravane took over as GOC Delhi Area; then again as Chief and Vice Chief; and eventually when Gen. Naravane took over as Chief of Army Staff from Gen. Rawat, who was appointed as India's first Chief of Defence Staff.

'I came in touch with Gen. Rawat quite late in life. It is surprising that despite serving the same organization, we had never met,' says Gen. Naravane. 'Both of us had been serving in different parts of the country till then.'

Gen. Rawat's posting to the east in 2013 had come as a surprise to a lot of people, since he had spent most of his time in Jammu and Kashmir. He had commanded his brigade and his division there. So when he got posted as the MGGS to Eastern Command, there were raised eyebrows and possibly also an apprehension as to how he would handle unfamiliar territory. All that was laid to rest soon enough.

'I remember seeing him for the first time at Dimapur in 2013, where the 3 Corps war game was going on,' says Gen. Naravane. 'He was attending as the MGGS designate. He had reported at Calcutta, though not yet taken over. There was no need for him to come for the war game, but he had come, which showed that he was willing to make an extra effort to familiarize himself with the demands of the new appointment.'

Gen. Naravane says that Gen. Rawat did not make an impression on him during that first meeting for two reasons. The first being that Gen. Rawat had just sat quietly through the entire exercise without any participation. And the second, Gen. Naravane remembers with a laugh, was this: Gen. Naravane was playing the enemy commander in the war game, the head of Yellow Land, and was naturally on his toes throughout, without any time to take impressions, especially since Gen. S.L. Narasimhan, then Corps Commander, and Gen. Dalbir Singh Suhag, then Army Commander, who later on went on to become Chief of Army Staff, were also attending.

'Despite being at such a senior position, Gen. Rawat just sat there quietly, observing and imbibing information. Since he had come to the east after a long time, he was obviously using the opportunity to relearn things and refamiliarize himself with the North-east,' recollects Gen. Naravane.

A few months later, the command war game took place in Calcutta, and Gen. Naravane was once again the 'enemy', with the four corps in the Eastern Command—3 Corps, 4 Corps, 33 Corps and 17 Corps—functioning as own troops. By then, Gen. Rawat was firmly in the chair. As MGGS, he was the lynchpin around whom the whole war game revolved. He had to see what the own forces (Blue Land) were doing, what the enemy forces (Yellow Land) were doing, match the whole thing and then decide the outcome.

This time he made a huge impression on everyone. 'Gen. Rawat was everywhere, without taking any breaks even for Saturday or

Sunday,' remembers Gen. Naravane. 'He knew the whole Command by then, which was remarkable, since it was a big command including a vast area, starting from Sikkim to the west, going up to Kibithu in the east, with Bhutan in the middle.'

## The Only Gift

Since Gen. Naravane was IG Assam Rifles for close to twenty-two months, he got to work with Gen. Rawat even when he was moved to Dimapur as Commander, 3 Corps. 'As luck would have it, I was still there, and that was the time he became my boss, and I worked closely with him for nearly eight months,' he says. So Naravane saw him as MGGS and then as Corps Commander. And from then on, the two were together almost all the time.

Naravane fondly remembers one particular dinner he hosted for Rawat in Kohima at end of 2014. 'Gen. Rawat had come on a visit, and we had a party for him in the mess that evening, where I pinned a small Naga spear lapel badge on his jacket.' That badge, he says, is the only gift he ever gave Gen. Rawat in all the years that they served together. And that was what Gen. Rawat appreciated the most. 'He did not believe in ostentatious gifts, and neither did I, so that became a connect between us,' says Gen. Naravane.

Gen. Rawat always advocated the view that material things didn't matter. 'If you want to impress me, impress me with work,' he would often say.

Naravane adds: 'I also remember him telling me once how someone had sent him a huge hamper for his birthday and how he had couriered it back to the concerned officer, at his own expense. He was really against the gifting culture.'

## Taking the Road Less Travelled

Naravane recollects an incident in Nagaland when Rawat had come to Kohima and, on his way back, insisted on driving from

Mokokchung to Tuensang, to see for himself the road that soldiers had to use. He had a helicopter, but he insisted on going by road, despite Naravane's efforts to make him reconsider. 'The roads in Nagaland are very bad. The road to Kohima is terrible, and Mokokchung to Tuensang was so bad that it took four painful hours to traverse the eighty-three-kilometre stretch. Since I had been visiting all my areas by road, I was aware of the road's condition and tried my best to dissuade him by saying, "Sir, *kyun road se ja rahe ho? Chopper se chalte hain* (Why are you going by road? Let's take the chopper)." But Gen. Rawat was insistent. He did not listen to me,' states Gen. Naravane.

'Unless I see it for myself, I will not come to know the situation on ground,' Gen. Rawat told him. '*Ek baar toh main road se jaunga hi jaunga* (I will definitely go by road at least once).'

And so the two generals did not ask for a chopper and took a Gypsy instead. It was four hours of backbreaking travel that both took in their stride. The road was in a terrible condition and riddled with deep potholes. Gen. Rawat was so appalled that midway he asked the driver, '*Gypsy ko iss khadde mein khadi karo, main ek photo lena chahta hun* (Stop the Gypsy in this pothole, I want to take a photo).'

The vehicle was parked in the pothole that, Gen. Naravane says, was so deep that almost the entire Gypsy went into it. Gen. Rawat then took a photograph, which he said he would send to the chief minister of Nagaland, to show him the state of his roads. 'I am quite sure he would have done it too,' says Gen. Naravane. 'He was not a man to take things lying down.'

## A Man of Action

That Bipin was not a man to take things lying down became obvious soon after. On 27 March 2015, when he was Commander, 3 Corps, the National Socialist Council of Nagaland (NSCN [K])—a Naga nationalist separatist group—abrogated its fourteen-year ceasefire with the Indian government. Two shocking ambushes took place in Nagaland. In the first one, a 23 Assam Rifles water bowser, going to a village stream to fetch water, was ambushed and fell victim to an IED—the attack led to the death of six people. In the second, an army convoy was ambushed in Chandel district, leading to the brutal killing of eighteen soldiers.

Naravane had left on posting when these happened but he says that in his final months in Nagaland, he had a gut feeling that the ceasefire was going to break. 'The signs were already there,' he says. 'A senior insurgent leader's son, who used to study in Sainik School, Punglwa, in the outskirts of Dimapur, did not rejoin school after the winter break, which implied that the insurgent leader was possibly moving his wife and children out of harm's way.'

It was also observed that the strength in certain militant camps, which the Assam Rifles used to keep under watch, was going down. 'The numbers had gone down from 100 to nineteen, which meant that the militant group had slowly started moving its cadres out,' Naravane explains. Militant camps were out of bounds for the forces while a ceasefire was in effect, but once the militants broke the ceasefire Assam Rifles could immediately launch an attack on the camps. A depleting strength in militant camps implied that the insurgents were slowly moving their cadres out of harm's way since they planned to break the ceasefire. 'All the pieces of the jigsaw were there,' says Gen. Naravane. 'Unfortunately, ambushes are very difficult to predict or prevent.'

Naravane was in Delhi when the attacks took place, but he says he has no doubts that Gen. Rawat would have strongly advocated striking back. 'He would not have taken it lying down. He would have definitely insisted on strong action,' Naravane says. And soon the Indian Army's retaliatory surgical strikes took place, where in a daring operation Indian para commandos crossed the border and struck militant camps in Myanmar getting the moral ascendency back.

* * *

## 'He Was Easy to Work With'

'Gen. Rawat was an easy man to work as well as converse with,' says Gen. Naravane, remembering his tenure as GOC when Bipin was his Corps Commander. 'There are Corps Commanders who want to micromanage everything, and I have seen people like that when I was COAS. But he never did that. He was not the kind to breathe down the necks of his GOCs, the divisional commanders. He understood it well that he should not be too hands-on and allow them to function in their own way. He let us do what we wanted to, without interference.'

The other quality that Naravane says he really appreciated in Rawat was his unflappable temperament. 'If there was an accident—for instance, if a vehicles had gone down the khud, or someone had died—we would have to give that report to the Corps Commander at the end of the day. There was never any overreaction from him. He would just take it in his stride. He would not say, "Sack the CO." He understood that when people are working every day and hundreds of vehicles are plying on the roads, one odd accident might happen. Making a mistake is a sign that people are working. If you sit inside your post and do nothing, you will naturally stay safe since nothing will happen.'

The same was visible to all when Gen. Rawat was onboard a helicopter that crashed in Dimapur. 'I was in Kohima. We heard that a hard landing had taken place,' recollects Gen. Naravane. 'He did not show any signs of fear or anger after the crash, and reassured the pilot, asking him not to worry, since accidents happen.'

After Dimapur, Gen. Bipin Rawat went to Pune as Army Commander, Southern Command, for about eight months, after which he returned to Delhi as Vice Chief of the Indian Army.

'I also had a short break in Delhi before I went to Command 2 Corps,' says Gen. Naravane. And then he was called back to Delhi as GOC, Delhi Area. 'I am sure he had a role to play in getting me to Delhi Area, but he never told me, and I also never asked him,' Gen. Naravane says.

After being promoted to Army Commander Grade, Gen. Naravane served as General Officer Commanding-in-Chief, Army Training Command, from December 2017 to September 2018. Thereafter, he served as General Officer Commanding-in-Chief, Eastern Command, from October 2018 to August 2019.

'He got me to Delhi Area first,' says Gen. Naravane. 'Then he sent me to Army Training Command (ARTRAC), in Shimla. After this he sent me to Eastern Command, and for his last four months in office as Chief, he got me as Vice Chief.'

Gen. Naravane says he had the honour to dine with Gen. Rawat as outgoing COAS, and in his speech as incoming COAS, Gen. Naravane gave his predecessor the last farewell in the Battle Honours Mess, in which he candidly stated that Gen. Rawat had been grooming him for the COAS job without telling him anything. Gen. Rawat just smiled at him from where he was sitting.

'He never said anything to me, and I never asked him anything,' Gen. Naravane states sincerely. 'But he made sure I saw more and more of the army in those years.'

Through the ARTRAC, Gen. Naravane says, he got the opportunity to see all the training establishments of the Indian Army, like the High Altitude Warfare School in Gulmarg, the Officers Training Academy in Chennai, the Electrical and Mechanical Engineering School in Baroda and the Counter-Insurgency and Jungle Warfare School (CIJWS) in Vairengte.

All this exposure helped him a lot, in terms of understanding the training requirements of the army. And, of course, his year as Army Commander was invaluable too. In his four months as Vice Chief, he says, he came to know the working of the Ministry of Defence and the bureaucracy. 'All the briefings I would have to take as Chief I got those as Vice Chief, so it was hands-on experience that prepared me for the task he was planning to give me, without giving a single hint.'

## A Warm, Affectionate Person

Gen. Naravane remembers Gen. Rawat as a warm and affectionate person. Rawat would make it a point to attend every wedding or raising day that anyone personally came to invite him for, and that was among his endearing qualities. 'He used to say that if somebody has come to my office and waited outside for half an hour to give me a card, then I have got to go for that wedding,' Gen. Naravane says.

Naravane recollects with a smile that he and Gen. Rawat, along with their wives, sometimes attended as many as three weddings in an evening during the wedding season in Delhi. Sometimes, two weddings and one raising day. 'He used to say, "We will have snacks at the first, dinner at the second and sweets at the third." And all four of us would be party-hopping till late evening.'

## Professional Disagreements

'When you work with someone, you are bound to have some professional disagreements,' says Gen. Naravane. 'You are dealing with so many issues as Chief and Vice Chief, or even as CDS and Chief, you tend to have differences of opinion sometimes. He might not have agreed with something in the first instance, but if you persisted and persevered, he would realize that the issue was important for you and you felt strongly about it. Then he would be willing to listen.'

## Modernizing the Army

One major contribution of Gen. Rawat, which was followed up by Gen. Naravane and which he hopes will shortly be put in place, is the concept of Integrated Battle Groups (IBG).

The IBG is aimed at shortening the decision-making loop in the Indian Army by reducing the links in between. The idea works on the belief that when the brigade and the division are merged, one link is removed in the chain of decision-making, and the loop becomes shorter, increasing efficiency. It was also felt that multiple headquarters had a role to play in the old times, when communication was poor and radio sets had a limited range. 'Now, sitting in Delhi, I can see what is happening in Sikkim. So we do not need so many links in the chain,' explains Gen. Naravane.

'Gen Rawat championed the cause in a big way, and I was very much in favour of it,' he says, recounting how, as GOC ARTRAC, he had himself made an independent presentation to the Army Commanders about having lighter divisions by merging the brigades and divisions.

'My idea was to have strong battalions, a light division and a corps,' he says. 'But when I presented it to the Army Commanders in 2018, it did not find much favour.' Incidentally, Gen. Rawat too had independently landed on the same idea. 'Our ideas converged. He started the project, gave it the nomenclature IBG, and I could follow it up. It is now a work-in-progress and is aimed at making us operationally more efficient.'

There is a discreet tap on the door of the study. It is Gen. Naravane's helper, politely reminding him that he has another appointment scheduled and his car is waiting. Excusing himself, the General gets up. 'I had a very good innings with Gen. Rawat but the end was very tragic,' he says, in the memory of the man who was instrumental in making him reach where he did. 'You would not wish an end like that for anyone.' And, with a final handshake, he is out of the door.

# 'He Was Garhwal's Hope for a Better Future'

8 December
Arun Vihar
Noida

Col Satpal Parmar was visiting his bank at the Ganga Shopping Complex when his cellphone started ringing. He ignored it, since he was busy withdrawing cash, but the calls kept coming. Exasperated, he reached out for his cell to check who was trying to contact him so desperately. It showed multiple missed calls from his brother-in-law Deepak Chauhan, who lived in Bangalore.

Col Parmar walked back to his car, and once he was comfortably seated inside, he called back. He was shocked to learn that his nephew Bipin Rawat's helicopter had crashed. '*Bhaisahab, aap ghar jaiye aur TV lagaiye* (Go home and switch on the TV),' Deepak said.

Col Satpal drove back as if in a trance, and entered his flat to find his wife and children sitting shell-shocked in front of the television set. The news channels were constantly flashing pictures and videos of Gen. Bipin Rawat, resplendent in his uniform, proud and upright, looking straight into the camera. Col Satpal could not believe the horrific news. He had met Bipin and Madhu for lunch just two days back. Telling his wife to pack a suitcase since they might have to fly to Wellington, he decided to drive down to Defence House, the official CDS residence on Kamraj Road.

On his way he kept trying Madhu's cell frantically, but it would not connect. Just as they crossed the Nizamuddin Bridge, he got a call from Lt Col Arati, staff officer to Madhulika. *'Sir, jaldi aaiye* (come quickly), we have not broken the news of the crash to Tarini,' she said. By then it had become clear that Madhulika was no more, but Bipin was believed to be alive though critical.

Around 2.15 p.m., when the Parmars got close to the CDS residence, Kamraj Road had been turned into a fortress. There were police barricades everywhere. Col Satpal saw Defence Minister Rajnath Singh's car entering the premises. 'At that moment, I just knew we had lost Bipin,' he says. 'Why else would the Defence Minister be at his house.'

As he waited in his car, to be allowed entry into the house, Col Satpal's mind was swamped by memories of his beloved nephew. He had been in class six when his sister Sushila had got six-month-old Bipin to the village. Everyone had fallen in love with the fat gurgling baby with pink cheeks who would keep smiling all the time. Bipin had been in school when collegiate Satpal went to stay with his sister in Dehradun and would make the gentle and obedient Bipin sit next to him and study till late into the night. *'Mamaji, bahut neend aa rahi hai. So jaayen?'* Bipin would ask softly, when he could no longer keep his eyes opem. And then a memory from just two years back flashed before his eyes. Bipin, now more friend than nephew, had called him up laughing and declared in his characteristic boisterous manner, *'Mama, chaar din baad gaon ja raha hun. Kisi ko pata nahi chalna chahiye* (Mama, I am going to the village four days later. No one should know).' Ignoring his wish completely, Satpal had immediately called up his other nephew who lived in Thati (their village) and told him, '*Beta Narender, Bipin gaon aa raha hai. Sara intezaam kar ke rakhna* (Narender, Bipin is coming to the village. Make all the preparations).'

\* \* \*

20 September 2019
Thati village
Dhanari block
Uttarkashi

The air rings out with the sounds of the dhol and damau, the drums played in the hills of Garhwal on all festive occasions. Loud cheers of 'Jai Hind' and 'Bipin Rawat ki jai' reverberate in the cold mountain air as the slim sticks in the hands of the two drummers meet the hide of the percussion instruments. Villagers line up with marigold garlands to receive the man of medium height and stocky build who stands in their midst, smiling widely. He is in uniform, wears a green beret and has collar dogs, from which four sparkling stars glint in the sun.

Chief of Army Staff Gen. Bipin Rawat is visiting his maternal grandfather the late Thakur Surat Singh Parmar's village in Uttarkashi. The General's wife stands by his side, accepting the warm greetings of the villagers. Bipin has flown in from Harsil and then driven 30 km from the ITBP helipad at Matli, where his chopper landed at 9.30 a.m. Over fifty-three years back, when he was brought to the village as a baby in his mother's lap, his parents had to cover the distance on horseback and in the *dandi*, the Pahadi version of a palanquin—a big wooden chair tied carried by four men.

Spread over 31 hectares and with 150 households, Thati is one of the main villages of the Dhanari block, which gets its name from its rich yield of *dhan* (rice). Dhanari is a cluster of forty-six villages, all of which used to come under Thakur Surat Singh, Bipin's grandfather, at that time. In the British period, Singh, a rich and well-respected man, was in charge of revenue collection for the entire block.

Located 32 km from Uttarkashi and nearly 150 km from Dehradun, Thati is based on the intersection of two rivers, Dhanpati and Kalgari, and is known for its Rajrajeshwari temple, which is the first place that Bipin visits. Paying his respects to the local deity, he walks down to his cousin Narender Parmar's house. Narender is Bipin's first cousin, the son of his mother's younger brother, Khushpal. There, he is affectionately fed the traditional daal ke pakode, a Garhwali delicacy, and given a priceless gift—an old photograph of him as a baby with his mother and his grandparents that was taken in Dhanari when he was brought there as a baby.

People want to touch him, make videos, take pictures with him, shake his hand, and he obliges them all. He is the son of the village, having visited it twice before—once as Second Lieutenant, when he had dragged his friend Rakesh Sharma along to show him his maternal village (the two of them were posted as Second Lieutenants in 5/11 GR in Harsil); and the first time as a six-month-old baby.

Col Satpal Parmar is the younger brother of Bipin's mother, Sushila. He is the mama who saw Bipin grow up in front of his eyes and proudly stayed by his side as he grew in age and rank, reaching one milestone after another.

Col Parmar looks at the family photograph that hangs in his Noida flat and fondly remembers the first time Bipin was brought to Thati as a baby. 'My sister Sushila visited the village after her elder son was born. There was no road in those times, and much of the journey had to be done on foot or on horseback,' he reminisces.

## Bipin's First Visit to Dhanari

September 1958

When Bipin was six months old, his mother, Sushila, decided she wanted to take him to the village to meet her parents. Capt.

Laxman Singh Rawat, who was posted in Dehradun, agreed to his wife's wishes, and the couple travelled to Dhanari with their firstborn, a happy gurgling Bunny, who would mostly be asleep in his mother's arms.

The young couple boarded a small Garhwal Motors bus from Dehradun that took them via Rishikesh, Narendra Nagar, Chamba and Tehri, to finally reach Dharasu, the last motorable point 30 km from the village. Thakur Surat Singh had sent up his horses and a dandi for his daughter and son-in-law. Many villagers also went up to the roadhead to receive Bade Thakur Sahab's grandson. The couple were received with respectful greetings of Jai Deo Maharaj and Dei Sahiba, offered hot tea and snacks, and then the procession made its way back to Thati, singing and chattering in excitement.

'It took them almost six hours to cover those thirty kilometres on foot,' remembers Col Parmar. 'I was also in the village at that time, studying in class sixth, in the government school that had been constructed by my chachaji, Thakur Krishna Singh, who had been Education Minister, and on land donated by his older brother, my father, Thakur Surat Singh. It catered to the educational needs of all the children in the nearby villages.'

Col Satpal has a smile on his face when he recollects the excitement that Bipin's arrival created. '*Bade Thakur Sahabak naati ayun cha* (Bade Thakur Sahab's grandson is here).' It made big news in the village. Children from nearby villages would come over to see him, and he was a delightful baby, with his pink chubby cheeks, sparkling eyes and a playful smile. He was handed over from one set of arms to another, and people instantly fell in love with him. 'Even the servants would fight for a turn to hold the baby.'

He says he clearly remembers the day the young Captain decided to depart, taking his pretty wife and son along. 'What a sight it was. Capt. Laxman Singh was on his horse, looking fit and handsome. Sushila Didi and Bipin were in a dandi. It was being carried by four men from the village, two in front and two behind. They were holding the wooden chair up in the air. All of us stood around waving goodbye. Many of the villagers accompanied the travellers to the roadhead, from where the young couple caught a bus back to Dehradun.'

For an emotional Sushila, who had left the village to study in Dehradun when she was six years old, the ride was reminiscent of the caravans the family would move in, back when there was no motorable road to Dhanari. Horses, dandis, servants and cooks would travel together all the way to and from Dehradun, making two halts in between—one at a place called Bhaneti and another at a place near Mussorie hills. Finally, on day three, the entire family would reach Dehradun, travel-weary but excited.

## 'Itna Soft Hai, Fauj Ka Ragda Kaise Lega?'

Col Satpal also remembers one of Bipin's early birthdays that was celebrated in Dehradun. 'It must have been his second or third birthday. I had been sent to Dehradun for my higher education and was studying in a Christian missionaries-run school in Paltan Bazaar. I had gone to attend the party, and I remember eating a lot and having a very good time, with Bipin as a toddler waddling around the house, still learning to walk properly.'

Bipin, he says, was a sweet and obedient child, the perfect role model for his younger siblings: Kiran, who was quite docile too, and Vijay, who was notoriously naughty right from childhood. Col Satpal shares memories of staying with his sister in their civil accommodation in Bindaal near Doon School, when Bipin and Vijay were in school and Satpal himself was in college. 'Since their father was not with them, I was told by the family to go and live with Sushila Didi. So I left our 14 New Road house and stayed with them for about seven months, till Didi moved with Jijaji and the children were put in boarding school,' he says.

During this period, he would often make Bipin sit up with him and study at night. 'When he was tired he would hesitantly ask me, "*Mamaji, neend aa rahi hai, ab so jaayen* (I am sleepy. Should we go to sleep)?" When I had visited them in Shimla, we would go for long walks, and Bipin was such a soft child that soon his cheeks would flush pink and he would say, "*Mamaji bahut thak gaye, chalo ghar wapis chalte hain* (I am tired. Let's go back home)." We would turn back and head home,' Col Satpal recounts, a smile playing upon his lips.

\* \* \*

Col Satpal remembers the time when he went on a holiday to Dalhousie, where then Brig. Rawat was posted as Brigade Commander, 323 Mountain Brigade. 'I had taken a train that dropped me off at Pathankot. From there I had to travel by road to Dalhousie. Suddenly, I looked up to find Bipin standing in front of me with a shy smile on his face. He was in eleventh standard at that time and had been sent to receive me at the railway station. "*Mamaji, main NDA ja raha hun* (I am joining the NDA)," he told me.'

Hearing this, Col Satpal was more worried than happy. 'I thought he was such a delicate child. How would he survive the tough army training? *Mujhe chinta thi ye fauj ka ragda kaise lega.*' He expressed the same doubt to his sister, who just smiled and said she was sure Bipin would be able to do it. And, as everyone would soon find out, she knew her son well. He was way tougher than people thought.

On 16 December 1978, Gentleman Cadet Bipin Rawat passed out of the Indian Military Academy, watched over by his proud parents, Gen. and Mrs Laxman Singh Rawat. Then Captain Satpal had come from Kashmir, where he was posted, to attend his nephew's passing out parade. 'Bipin was the recipient of the Sword of Honour. It was a proud day for the family. I was amazed to see his transformation, from a frail kid to this fit and handsome young officer. He had changed completely. The chubby cheeks were gone, his face had become well chiselled, he had become so much taller. He looked strong and confident,' says Col Satpal, a nostalgic look in his eyes.

Lt Gen. Gajendra Singh Rawat was the Commandant of the Indian Military Academy when Bipin Rawat graduated. 'Though the surname was the same, he was not a relative,' says Col Satpal, alluding to gossip that had been doing the rounds in social media, hinting that the Sword of Honour came to Bipin because he was related to the then IMA Commandant. 'Many years later, our cousin Beena Didi's daughter Archana was married to Gen. G.S. Rawat's son Jitender, but back in 1978 no one knew that was going to happen. There was absolutely no relation at that time. Fact is that Bipin did very well in the academy. The Sword of Honour is not given on the IMA Commandant's whim and fancy. It has to be earned by a GC, who is observed during the entire period of training. No way can it be manipulated,' he says.

Col Satpal says malicious gossip about Bipin started doing the rounds after he became Chief of Army Staff. 'He was a tough chief, who took some harsh decisions. He was a straightforward man himself and applied the same rules to others. He did not let anyone indulge in any kind of corruption. He brought in many changes, and since he was a strict disciplinarian, he ensured that these were applied strictly. Change is always resisted. Bipin had withdrawn all unnecessary sahayaks serving with retired people, and many obsolete perks and privileges that are a part of the army's colonial legacy.'

Col Satpal insists that soldiers understood that Bipin always had their welfare in mind. 'Ask the jawans, and they will tell you how much he cared for them. His orders were, "Look after your men, give them facilities, make a difference to their lives." But yes, he was tough with senior officers. This was not liked by people and is the reason why many started lobbying against him.'

\* \* \*

That day in 2019, when Bipin drove into the village fulfilling a wish he had harboured for many years, as many as 700 Garhwalis from around the area collected there to see the son of Thati. Their chests swelled with pride that one of their own had reached the top of his career, and was wearing his fame and accomplishment so humbly. He became an instantaneous hero to every village boy seeking a career in the forces. They followed him when he walked across to Panchpura, his grandfather's five-storey house made of wood and stone. They smiled as he made himself comfortable on a cheap plastic chair and sipped a cup of tea, reaching out for the home-made daal ke pakode, telling his cousin's family that they were the best he had ever eaten. They hung upon his every word as he spoke of roads being a sign of progress, and they believed him when he said he dreamt of facilitating the construction of good medical and engineering colleges in Garhwal to stop *palayan* (migration from villages to the city). He was their hope for a better future. Unfortunately, he could not live long enough to fulfil those dreams.

# 'My Father Was a Simple Man'

8 December 2021
Day of the accident
Delhi District Court
Post noon

Twenty-eight-year-old Tarini Rawat, a lawyer by profession, had finished her work for the day and was getting back from court, not really looking forward to going home, since she knew her parents would not be there. They had left that morning for Sulur in Tamil Nadu, from where they were to go to Wellington, where her father, Gen. Bipin Rawat, had an official engagement. They must have reached by now, she thought, smiling as she remembered how excited her mother had been the night before about meeting old friends on that trip. She absent-mindedly reached for her cell and was surprised to find the many WhatsApp notifications on the screen. They appeared to be mentioning a helicopter crash. Tarini just glanced at one in curiosity. And suddenly, her whole world went blank. The crashed helicopter had been carrying her parents.

## Meeting Tarini

17 May 2022
Dhaula Kuan
New Delhi

Tall, fair, bespectacled Tarini Rawat opens the door to the flat she
has shifted into from Defence House, where she had been living with
her parents. There is a gentle smile on her young face. For a twenty-
nine-year-old who lost both her parents just six months back, she is
remarkably composed. She sits in front of their photograph, wearing
a suit that belonged to her mother, and talks about the two people
who loved her the most in life.

Behind her, they smile from a framed portrait: Gen. Rawat, with
his salt-and-pepper hair, looking handsome in a black bandgala; Mrs
Madhulika Rawat in an off-white silk sari draped gracefully over her
shoulders, a string of pearls around her neck.

'My mother always dressed very well, and she would often share
clothes with me, since we were almost the same size,' Tarini says.
'These days I wear her salwar kameez all the time.' That is the only
admission she makes to her emotional state. She is missing her
parents but is too dignified to make that loss public.

## Memories from Kritika's Marriage

Tarini says some of her fondest memories of her parents are from
the time when her elder sister, Kritika, got married. The match had
been fixed in late 2016, soon after Gen. Rawat had shifted to Delhi
from Pune to take over as Vice Chief. The boy, Ankit Singh, had
been suggested by a common friend and had completely met the
family's expectations. He was from a business family that owned
dye and textile factories in Mumbai. 'My father and sister approved
of Ankit. Mom and I liked him too,' she says. The marriage got
finalized in November, and very soon after that, on 17 December,

it was announced that Gen. Bipin Rawat would be the next Chief of Army Staff. In January 2017, he took over, and, by the end of the month, the Rawats shifted from 25 Safdarjung Road, the official residence of the Vice Chief, to Army House, the Chief's residence, at 4 Rajaji Marg.

The marriage was fixed for 5 March, just five days short of Kritika's thirtieth birthday. Tarini laughs about how pleased Kritika was about getting married before she turned thirty. Tarini remembers how chaotic it became for her mother, since she had just taken over as first lady and also president of the Army Wives Welfare Association (AWWA) and had a lot of responsibilities to handle.

'In January she had to host the Army Day banquet in Chief's house. In February she had to host a garden party for the wives of serving officers. And in March there was the wedding,' Tarini recounts. 'Mom got really busy.'

Life changed for her father even more. Foremost to be addressed were security issues. He could no longer drive his own car, so the silver-grey Maruti Suzuki Dzire, which he had replaced his earlier grey Zen with, had to go into the garage. He could no longer accompany his family for meals to restaurants. He had to always move with security cover. And he became extremely busy with the pressures of the appointment. He had always been a workaholic, but now the job came with even more demands on his time.

In spite of his new position, Kritika's wedding was one time when she saw her dad really excited, she says. That was the only time she remembers when he took so much interest in what he was going to wear. 'Mom had ordered some gold-plated buttons for a sherwani for the groom. When Papa saw the buttons, he liked them so much that he said he was taking them for his own sherwani. Mom had to order some more for Ankit,' she shares with a nostalgic smile.

He wore a well-fitted bandgala, with the gold buttons he had taken a fancy to, and an elegant *safa*, looking handsome and happy, with Madhulika standing by his side in a beautiful yellow sari. Tarini wore an orange Rajput *poshak*, and Kritika, the bride, was stunningly attired in her mother's red wedding poshak that had specially been restitched and refitted for her. For the family, it was a moment to be cherished.

Other than the wedding, Tarini says she has very few memories of her father at family events. 'He did not celebrate his birthday, and even on our birthdays we did not do anything very special. We didn't go out too often as a family, because he would be so busy, and also, he liked his dal, chawal and sabzi meals—the regular *ghar ka khana*. My father was a simple man.'

## 'If He Could, He Would Have Gone to Office Even on Weekends'

Tarini remembers her father as a man who worked really hard and, in spite of the high appointments he held, stayed in touch with his roots. He was building a house in Dehradun, where he planned to settle down after retirement, dreaming of spending evenings on a rocking chair with a shawl draped over his shoulders. He was also learning to speak Garhwali, which he could understand well. 'He would search for funny Garhwali videos on YouTube and watch them in bed after an early dinner,' she says. He would also practise the Garhwali he was picking up online with Garhwali-speaking people.

On 1 December 2021, when Gen. Bipin Rawat was invited to Srinagar in Pauri Garhwal to attend the ninth convocation of the Hemvati Nandan Bahuguna Garhwal University, he made time for it despite his busy schedule. Wearing a dark-blue robe and hat, he addressed the gathering, starting with a Garhwali phrase. '*Sahmanya dagdaiyon* (respected friends),' he said with a smile, much to the delight of the faculty members and students, and then added that since it was a central university, he would now be speaking in Hindi and English. He went on to tell the students that he felt very nostalgic standing before them, that he considered their university his own alma mater, since he too belonged to Garhwal; and he then went on to passionately tell them about failure, and how it should be used as a learning and a stepping stone to success.

'We have seen him relaxed. We have seen him upset and frustrated. But we never saw him discussing work. The bottom line was that he would bring work home but never bothered us with work-related issues. He always had a study in every house we stayed in, where he would sit and do his office work. If he could, he would have gone to office even on weekends,' says Tarini with a laugh.

But after he became Chief, he stopped going to work on holidays, because had he done that, the entire office staff would have also had to come. He did not want to bother them and would work from his home office, often sitting there for hours, engrossed in work, dressed in his khadi kurta pajama—kurtas that were mostly bought by his wife, who would pick them up from Khadi Bhandar.

Tarini says her father had simple tastes when it came to clothes. She mostly remembers him in his light-coloured shirts and trousers, PT rig or the kurta pajamas that he would wear at home. 'Clothes were the last thing on his mind,' she says. 'If he needed anything, he would ask his buddies to get it from the Cantonment market, and they would just go and buy stuff. Mom would sometimes get a little irritated, and she would go to Khadi Bhandar and pick up kurtas in pastel shades for him.'

Tarini remembers how her father used to watch comedy shows to let off steam after work. 'Generally, after dinner, he would change into his kurta pajama, switch on his television and watch Tata Sky, which had a channel reserved exclusively for comedy,' she says.

Talent-hunt shows like *Little Champs* or *Dance India Dance*, and others on music and dance would also interest him, and if a particular participant had really impressed him, he would tell the family about him or her, asking them to watch the show too.

## Torpedoes Shooting around His House

Bipin Rawat loved his dogs. They were his family, and Tarini says there were no rules for them. 'When we were in our Noida house, they would often jump on his bed and refuse to get off, so he would go to sleep with them cuddled around him,' she recounts, adding though, that when her mother had decided to bring home their first dog, Ginger, a dachshund, her father had been completely against it.

Madhulika had always had dogs in her house when she was growing up and had decided that her family was incomplete without one. Though Bipin was against getting a dog, she overruled him and brought home a dachshund puppy that she named Ginger. 'Eventually, Dad was the one who started pampering Ginger the most,' Tarini says with a smile.

Soon after, they got Dash, another dachshund. When Ginger died, Dash got lonely and started getting depressed, and the Rawats decided to get him company. 'We adopted Tickle, a ten-month-old dachshund, through the Society for Prevention of Cruelty towards Animals,' Tarini says.

The youngest, Bailey, came when the family was living in the Chief's house. 'Dash had gotten really old, and we got him as a replacement in advance,' says Tarini. The dogs were his stress-busters and much-loved members of the family. They could barge into his television interviews and scamper around him when he was talking to guests.

The first interview he gave as Chief, while still living in the official residence of the Vice Chief, was to journalist Sandeep Unnithan, who mentions Dash and Tickle, dressed in red-and-black trimmed winter fleece, shooting around him like twin torpedoes while a fleet of black armoured Scorpios waited to take Bipin to his South Block office.

Tarini remembers how, during an Aaj Tak interaction with journalist Manjeet Negi, Dash, Tickle and Bailey—returning from a walk—had caught sight of Gen. Rawat, barged past the cameramen and run up to him, while the interview was going on. The cameras had to be stopped and restarted after the General had petted all three and sent them off.

## Mamma and Her John Denver Songs

Tarini says that since her father was mostly serving in field areas and, later on, busy in his very prestigious appointments, she has more memories of her mother than of him. Madhulika was the one the girls spent most of their time with. She likes to point out that though both her parents were completely different people, they were quite similar in many ways. 'They were both social and outgoing, and enjoyed interacting with people. My mother would set time aside to meet her college friends and keep her schedule open for people. Papa kept busy, but there would never be any awkwardness when he met a new person. If he did not know you, he would try to know you better. He was genuinely interested in other people.'

They both liked music as well. 'Mamma liked old music, from Hindi films, as well as classics like the Beatles and John Denver. She would give me lists to download for her. When Nani was with us during the Covid lockdown, Mamma had bought a Caravan radio for her. So, through the day, we would have old Hindi film songs playing in the house, and we would be humming along with them,' she says.

Her father's music choice would keep changing, Tarini says. Sometimes he would be listening to Sufi songs, at other times Gorkhali folk songs. Though he was not a great singer, he would happily take the mic and sing Nepali songs with his troops, cracking jokes and dancing with them at *badakhanas*. He could sit on his haunches with arms akimbo and do the jhamre dance, throwing his legs in the air effortlessly. Bipin spoke fluent Gorkhali as well. Madhulika and the girls had picked it up too.

'Mamma loved to travel,' says Tarini. Though she had stayed in Noida with her in-laws when the children were younger and Bipin was doing his Kashmir and Congo tenures, after the girls grew up Madhulika would be by his side during most of his work-related travel. If she was flying with him, she would make videos of the landscape below and send those to the family.

'Sometimes, she would even record the pilot announcing where they were flying and which ghats or river they were crossing. She would always involve us in whatever she was doing, wherever she was,' says Tarini.

Madhulika was a hands-on mother who always had time for her family. She would display her affection for her daughters at every chance she got. She would take them for movies, stitch clothes for them, celebrate their achievements and handle their disappointments. She would share with them jokes, emotions and fashion advice, along with her best saris and her favourite John Denver songs. And she is gone now. But she has left behind a heart full of memories that no one can take from them and a closet full of clothes that still smell of her perfume. 'I wear them all the time. It's like I still have her around me,' says Tarini, with a smile.

# 'Sahab Ko Toh Aaj Hero Ban Ke Hi Jana Hai'

8 December 2021
P-94 A, Shankar Vihar
New Delhi
7.15 a.m.

Geetika Lidder had just completed her morning puja when she heard her husband's raised voice. Brigadier Lakhbinder Singh Lidder, SM, VSM, had a heart of gold but a short temper. He appeared annoyed. '*Uniform pe normal lanyard kyun lagaaya hua hai* (Why have you attached a normal lanyard [cord worn around the shoulder] on the uniform)?' he was asking his sahayak, Rohit. '*Aaj aglets lagaane the* (Today aglets [ceremonial braided cord with metal] had to be attached).'

Geetika rushed to Rohit's rescue. 'Toni, *humein kya pata aapki uniform mein kaunse din kya lagaana hota hai* (How do we know what attach to your uniform when),' she reasoned. '*Jab hum aglets lagaa ke rakhte hain, aap bolte ho, Dulha bana ke bhej dete ho. Lanyard*

181

*lagaya karo* (When we attach aglets, you say, Don't send me dressed like a bridegroom).'

Brig. Lidder had cooled down by then. '*Aaj change karne ka time hi nahi hoga* (I won't get time to change today). The chopper will land at Wellington, and we will go straight for the lecture,' he said.

'Aglets *laga do bhaiya. Sahab ko toh aaj hero ban ke hi jana hai* (Sahab wants to go dressed as a hero today),' Geetika told the relieved sahayak, smiling at her husband as she left the room.

A few hours later, Brig. Lidder was on a chopper bound for Wellington. He was in his ceremonial dress: stars shining, aglets sparkling, boots brushed to a subtle sheen. The chopper was destined never to reach its destination.

* * *

'I have played those lines in my mind so many times,' says Geetika Lidder, sipping from a steaming-hot cup of tea in the beautifully done-up house, where she now lives with her dog, Peeva, daughter, Aashna, and memories of her beloved husband of twenty-five years, who walked out of the door that morning after kissing her on the cheek and did not return.

She remembers affectionately how the late Brig. Lakhbinder, or Toni, as she used to call him, always took much pride in his fitness and how he was turned out. 'He left the house for the last time in his uniform, so fit, so well-dressed, looking as handsome as ever. That was how he lived and that's how he would have wanted to go,' she says, a fond smile playing on her lips.

Geetika says she would always see Toni off at the door and then wave him goodbye from the balcony as he got into his car and disappeared from view, and would turn the Buddhist prayer wheel fixed on the wall as she came back in. 'That day, I was taking an online class from 8.15 a.m. to 8.30 a.m., and so I didn't go out to see him off. I just put my video off when it was time for him to go. He gave me the customary peck on the cheek, and I told him, "*Aashna ko utha dena, uska exam hai* (Wake Aashna up. It's her exam).'' And I went back to my class.' Geetika was teaching class five at The Shri Ram School.

Brig. Lakhbinder used to carry two cellphones with him all the time, and he would stay in touch on WhatsApp. 'Landed at Coimbatore, boarding for Coonoor,' said a message he'd sent Geetika around 11.48 a.m., from one of his cells. 'Enjoy Wellington, it has given us so much,' she had replied, remembering how Toni had won the Scudder there, and how she had won the Navy Queen and danced with Gen. Sam Manekshaw. 'We both made some very special friends there, and I conceived Aashna. Wellington had been special for us,' she says.

Earlier that day, while going to ask the cook to make another round of tea that her husband had asked for, she had run into Gen. Rawat's bodyguards, the young smiling commandos who were also travelling to Wellington in the same chopper. They had dropped by on the way to the airport to pick up Lakhbinder's luggage, as they always did before a flight. It would be placed in the plane earlier, so that no time was wasted while boarding at Palam.

'*Chhutti ja rahe ho, bhaiya* (Are you going on a holiday)?' she had asked the one standing at the entrance. He had smiled and nodded. '*Hanji, ma'am, kal Wellington se wapis aayenge, agle din Indian Military Academy aur phir Saturday se chhutti* (We return from Wellington tomorrow and the next day it's Military Academy, and then I am on a holiday from Saturday).'

And the evening before, Geetika had gone across to Defence House to meet Madhulika Rawat.

\* \* \*

7 December 2021
Defence House
6 p.m.

Slim, dark-haired, attractive Geetika Lidder had left the house and was walking across to the staff entry where her car was parked. She had spent close to two hours with Madhulika Rawat, briefing her on whom she was expected to meet in Wellington, what gifts needed to be carried and what protocol needed to be followed. Being the Defence Assistant's wife, she routinely did this for all official trips made by the lady.

Their interaction was warm and pleasant, as always. Geetika then walked across to her car, her mind already on Aashna, her sixteen-year-old daughter, who had a board exam the next day. She caught sight of a Zomato bike parked near the gate of Defence House and joked in Gorkhali with the guards on duty, '*Ketaharu Zomato ma kin yati dhaire paisa kharch garchan* (Why do the boys spend so much money on Zomato)?' Since 2 JAK RIF, Lakhbinder's unit, had two Gorkha companies, Geetika had learnt to speak Gorkhali.

The guard laughed and said, '*Langar ko food ramro chai na, memsahib* (Langar food is not too great, ma'am)'. Geetika smiled and sat in the waiting car. In fifteen minutes she was home. She knew Toni would not be back before 9 p.m.

Checking on Aashna, who was studying, Geetika changed into her night suit, leant back on to the pillows and thanked god for all the gifts life had bestowed on her, the biggest among them being her husband, Toni, whom she had met when she was seventeen and he a newly commissioned officer in the Indian Army. Tall and handsome, he had swept her off her feet when she was still at school, and ever since he had been the most precious thing in her life. Geetika breathed a sigh of contentment and got engrossed in the book she had been reading.

* * *

'If he is watching, he should know that his girls are fine'

When she thinks back, Geetika says she often remembers the conversation she had with her husband the morning he left. The Lidders had been sitting together, having their second cup of tea, when, out of the blue, Lakhbinder had looked at her tenderly and said, 'You know what, Geets? Your God has been really kind to us. We always got more than we thought about.'

'Now when I look back, that was such a nice message he gave me,' she reminisces. 'He told me he was happy and contented.' It had been a rare admission of faith by a man who was not much of a believer. Geetika was the one to start her day with prayers.

She confesses that her life as an infantry man's wife was stressful. 'Every patrol he went for would weigh on my mind, and I would wait for him to get home safe. I would be fasting twice a week, even three times if he was in a field posting. All I prayed for was his happiness and safety.'

But lately, the strain had eased off. Toni had been promoted to the rank of Major General and was to join as General Officer Commanding somewhere in J&K in a month's time. 'He had reached a position where I could breathe easy. I had become complacent, since I felt he was no longer going to do assignments that would put his life at risk,' she says with a wry smile.

The night before she had fleetingly asked Toni to stay back. 'Must you go?' she had asked. 'It's getting very hectic for you. Besides, your brother is leaving for Canada on the tenth.'

He had replied, '*Bas ye last hi toh hai* (This is the last one). Gen. Rawat should not feel I am in the PONY [posted out not interested] mood.'

\* \* \*

8 December 2021
1.30 p.m.

Geetika was at an online school meeting with her phone on silent mode when she noticed an incoming call. It was from Brig. Anil Pundir, who happened to be a close friend of the family. She ignored it and continued with the meeting. A few minutes later, the call flashed again. Geetika ignored it one more time. But when the cell vibrated for the third time, she muted herself at the meeting and took the call.

'Ma'am, *TV dekh rahe ho* (Are you watching TV)?' Anil asked.

A puzzled Geetika replied, '*Nahi, Anil, TV kahan dekh rahi hun* (No, I am not watching TV). I am in a meeting.'

'Has Sir gone along with CDS?' Anil asked.

'Yes, he has,' an exasperated Geetika replied, wanting to get back to work.

'Ma'am, there has been a small accident,' Anil said. He sounded worried.

Soon, the house started filling up with people. Both her *maasis* had reached. Geetika was surprised to find one of them calling up her mother and saying, '*Achaa aap chale nahi ho* (Haven't you left)?'

'*Aap unko kyun bula rahe ho, Maasi. Abhi toh gaye the* (Why are you calling them, Maasi. They'd just left). They are old, they can't travel so much. If Toni is hurt, I might have to go to Wellington tomorrow,' Geetika found herself saying.

Since her parents had been in Delhi most of November, she did not want to trouble them again. From 1–14 November, they had stayed with Aashna, while Toni and Geetika had done a Prague trip with Gen. and Mrs Rawat. Later they had come again for the Lidders' twenty-fifth wedding anniversary and then for Aashna's book launch.

'I was not being allowed to watch TV, and I never thought that it was so serious,' she says.

Soon, people from her school also started collecting in the house. Her school principal and director were both there, as were other friends and colleagues. People were talking in whispers around her. A worried Geetika had tried to get in touch with her husband's NDC course mate at Wellington, but he did not take her call. She had also called the CDS exchange, pleading with them, '*Meri kisi bhi Deputy Defence Assistant Sahab se baat kara do* (Let me speak to any of the Defence Assistant Sahabs).' There were three of those—one each from the army, navy and air force. The exchange had told her, '*Ma'am, koi nahi mil raha, sab busy hain* (All are busy).' She had then called up Staff Officer Lt Col Aarti, who told her, '*Ma'am, kuch pata nahi chal raha. Main Tarini ke saath hun* (We still don't know the details. I am with Tarini).'

By evening, Veena Naravane, wife of COAS Gen. M.M. Naravane, had also come over, which made Geetika wonder, '*Itne bade log yahan kyun aa gaye hain* (Why are such important people coming here).'

'I kept thinking, *Accident ho gaya toh kya hua. Theek ho jayenge* (So what if he has had an accident. He will soon be better),' she says.

Mrs Naravane told her that there were three survivors.

'Why is it so difficult to identify him,' she asked him. 'He must be the tallest there.'

Around 5 p.m., timed with the Defence Minister's visit to Defence House, where he offered his condolences to Tarini, the Deputy Defence Attaché, Indian Navy, Captain Robin Chakravarty, came to Geetika, who was sitting on her bed with a *maala* in her hand, looking completely confused. He was in uniform. In the presence of Mrs Naravane, Robin took off his cap and broke the news to Geetika, saying, 'Ma'am, he was the nicest man I knew.'

Geetika says she does not remember what happened next, but possibly she broke down and then went looking for Anil, who was her comfort space at that point in time. She remembers telling people, '*I wish chot lag jaati, main sab dekh leti, main sab kar leti* (I wish he were wounded, I would have taken care of everything). *Main business kar leti* (I would have started a business). But there should have been life. With him I could do anything, not without him.'

Around 1.30 a.m., her parents had also reached the house from Chandigarh. 'It was very tough to see them,' she says. 'They were inconsolable.'

Geetika had been given Alprax injections, but she could not get to sleep. All night she kept wandering around the house followed by Peeva, telling Rohit, their sahayak, to take away all the saris she had collected over the years. '*Itni saari ikatthi kar li hain. Ab main kahan pehnungi, Rohit? Tum le jana* (So many have been collected. Where will I wear these now? You take them),' she repeatedly told him.

She asked people gathered in the lawn why they had come over when it was so cold and told them to go back to their homes. She met Aashna a few times, but it was only after everyone had left that she sat down with Aashna, and the two of them grieved for what they had lost. 'We just could not understand the way forward or what was going to happen to us. All my thought were centered around: How could this happen to us? How could he go? How could he do this?' she remembers.

The next morning Geetika went for her bath, where she let her tears flow freely, tricking down her face with the bath water. When she came out, she was completely composed. She found the house echoing with the loud wails of her mother, who was thumping her forehead in sadness, frustration and anger.

'She was constantly going, "*Humara bachcha itna achcha hai. Uske saath aisa kaise ho gaya* (Our child is so good. How could this happen to her)?" By then I had made peace with my god, and I told her, "*Ab to ye ho gaya na mere saath* (Now this has happened with me). Now, there is no why. Let's see how we will go on, but we have to stop cursing destiny."'

After that, she says, she cried only in the privacy of her bedroom, having decided that she would not make a public spectacle of her grief. 'My mother-in-law was inconsolable. She did not deserve this. I did not deserve this. None of us deserved it, but it happened. It was our destiny, and we have to live with it in the best possible way we can.'

\* \* \*

9 December 2021
Shankar Vihar

Geetika went across to Defence House to see how Tarini, Kritika and Agnes, wife of Lt Col Harjinder Singh, were doing. 'I knew

I had to see them. We were in it together,' she says. Bound by a common sense of deep loss, all four stood together at that tough time, handling their grief with remarkable stoicism. The entire day went waiting for the bodies to be brought back. Finally, around 7.30 p.m., two members from each family were asked to come to Palam to receive their loved ones. Geetika went across to Aashna and told her that her father was a much-respected man. 'I have always felt very proud of who we are and who he is, even when he was a Captain. So I told her we had no reason to let him down, and we were not going to make a public spectacle of ourselves So you'd better brace up and dress up.'

A devastated Aashna insisted that she would go to the airport as she was. But Geetika was firm. 'You will go as your father would have liked to see you,' she said, making her daughter wear her coat, trousers and scarf. She then opened her own box of saris and took out a nice silk sari, put on some light make-up and did her hair. 'I went to Palam as Mrs Lidder should have gone. It was a defining moment,' she says.

When the families reached Palam, the night was cold. Geetika says her teeth were chattering. The Prime Minister had come there to offer condolences. Kritika and Tarini were completely composed. Like typical military daughters, they handled their grief with the utmost dignity, as did Agnes. Preet, their teenage daughter, was quite numb. 'Overall, it was a hard day, but I think we held up well,' Geetika says.

The toughest moment for her was to see the coffin, with 'Brig. L.S. Lidder' written on it. 'I felt, there is the man I love. I wish I had enough to hold him or touch a hand. There was no closure there. It is something I will always miss.'

The last rites were to be done the next morning at Brar Square, but Geetika insisted that the coffin be brought home before that. 'We got flowers and did up the house. We brought him home. I wanted Peeva to see him. There was not much that you could see in the coffin, but he did come home, and I am proud of the fact that I didn't break down. And because I didn't, my daughter didn't. I think she was completely mirroring my behaviour. All the time her eyes were on me.'

She adds, 'I always told him that he had brought me up to be exactly the way he wanted. In his last moments also, I was exactly the way he would have liked . . . What has happened with me and my daughter is very harsh. Toni wouldn't have liked us to struggle. He wouldn't have liked me to draw a pension at forty-eight. We had plans to travel, to enjoy life, to be an interesting old couple. That was not to be. However, he has left enough love around us. Grief is private and we have kept it that way. I think I outdo myself to be happy, to look happy, to party with my friends, to keep the house as it used to be. If he is watching, he should know that his girls are fine.'

# 'Hum Ja Rahe Hain, Beta': Tarini's Last Memory

7 December 2021
Defence House, Kamraj Road
New Delhi
8 p.m.

Tarini, the younger of the Rawats' two daughters, was in her bed, a pillow propped up behind her back, reading a book with a cozy mink blanket pulled up to her chin, when she heard her mother call out. Madhulika was holding up a clothes hanger displaying her new sari with one hand, the other resting on her waist, curved fingers crinkling the folds of her soft cotton kaftan. '*Main Wellington mein ye sari pehenne wali hun kal* (I will be wearing this sari in Wellington tomorrow). What colour blouse will look good with this?' she asked, a frown creasing her forehead.

Tarini, who was a practising lawyer at the Delhi District Court, had lately become her mom's fashion consultant. Putting her book face-down beside her pillow, she pushed her glasses further up her nose and, swinging her legs off the bed, walked across to the dressing room that connected her bedroom to her parents'. Her mother stood with an open suitcase, packing for her two-day trip to Wellington, where Gen. Bipin Rawat had to deliver a lecture.

Tarini could see her dad through the half-open door on the other side. He was in his khadi kurta pajama, leaning back on the headboard of his bed, arms folded behind his head, one knee resting on another, deeply engrossed in watching the news on television. His suitcase had already been packed by his sahayaks. The uniform he was to wear the next morning had been neatly ironed and hung in his cupboard, medals rubbed to a sparkle. His polished boots were in the shoe rack.

The Rawats were flying to Wellington the next morning on an Indian Air Force plane that would take them from Palam to Sulur, from where another helicopter would take them to Wellington. The General had had a long day at work. He had returned from office late in the evening. When he walked in, Tarini sat in the room playing with the dogs. He had smiled at her and patted Bailey the dachshund, who had run across to him, wagging its tail.

The family had an early dinner of sandwiches and soup at 7 p.m., after which Bipin settled down to watch television while Madhulika opened her cupboard and got busy with packing. She was a little worried about the busy schedule, since she did not like leaving Tarini alone for too long. They were to return on 9 December and then go to Dehradun to attend the passing out parade at the Indian Military Academy, where Gen. Rawat had been invited as chief guest.

Tarini frowned in concentration, looking at the two blouses her mom was holding up against her sari. '*Ye better lagega* (This one will look better),' she said, picking one.

Madhulika folded it neatly and packed it in her suitcase obediently, smiling at her younger daughter. 'I am so looking forward to meeting Gen. and Mrs Anbu,' Madhulika said, her eyes sparkling. Lieutenant General Devraj Anbu, PVSM, UYSM, AVSM, YSM, SM, ADC, former Vice Chief of Army Staff (VCOAS), had retired from service in 2019 and settled down in Wellington. Madhulika was very close to the couple and was planning to spend an afternoon with them.

Tarini yawned.

'*Achha ab ja ke so ja* (Now go and sleep). I shall wake you up when we are leaving,' Madhulika said, looking over her shoulder affectionately.

Tarini trod back to her bed. She was still reading when, from the corner of her eye, she noticed her mom shutting the small suitcase which she was planning to take as cabin baggage and clicking the number lock in place. She had then switched off the dressing-room light and gone to her bedroom, gently pulling the connecting door shut behind her. Tarini could spot a chink of yellow light slipping in through the gap at the bottom of her parents' bedroom door.

She knew Dad must have fallen asleep watching television, since he had come back home so tired. Mom must have brushed her teeth and applied her night cream. Tarini thought she could hear the soft thuds of her feet walking back to her side of the bed. She imagined her mother leaning across to remove Dad's spectacles and pushing his fluffed-up pillow down so that he did not twist his neck and wake up with a crick. She must have pulled up the blanket and snuggled down into the pillows, turning to her left, which was how she usually slept, and reaching out to switch off her bedside lamp. There was a gentle click and, suddenly, the dressing room too was plunged into darkness.

Tarini read for a little while longer, soaking in the comfort of her parents' affection that seeped into her room even through the closed door and thick walls. Soon, her eyelids got heavy, and she started missing entire sentences. She found herself rereading the same lines again and again, and decided she was too sleepy to read any longer. Marking the page she was reading, she placed the book on her side table, switched off her lamp and closed her eyes. Within seconds she was asleep.

\* \* \*

8 December 2021
8.45 a.m.

'I vaguely remember Mom ruffling my hair in the morning while I was still in deep sleep. "*Hum ja rahe hain, beta* (We are leaving)," she said. I just mumbled bye and went back to sleep. She would always wake me up when she was going somewhere,' Tarini remembers.

She says she did not see her dad since he had already changed and was probably outside, discussing official engagements with his staff officers. The Rawats had a guest that morning: Subedar Major Bhisma Shrestha, from 5/11 GR, who had retired on 30 November. Since he had also served with Gen. Rawat as his Aide-de-Corps 2 (ADC2), he had come over with his wife, Amrita, to say goodbye. The General would never say no to anyone who wished to see him, and soldiers from the regiment were very special. Both Bipin and Madhulika met the Nepali couple with a lot of affection, and Bipin spoke to them in flawless Gorkhali. He asked about their health, their post-retirement plans and how their children were doing.

Shrestha Sahab requested him for a photograph, and the couple readily agreed. The four of them had a picture taken together and, after having a cup of tea with their guests, Gen. and Mrs Rawat left. That was to be the last picture of the CDS and his wife. Tarini has it now, since it was sent to her by one of the General's staff officers. In the photo, her father stands upright, resplendent in his uniform, and her mother stands by his side in a dark-blue salwar kameez, looking peaceful and relaxed. The Shresthas are beside them, smiling into the camera.

Dash, Tickle and Bailey, the three family dachshunds, were scampering around the house when the photo was being taken, annoyed that they were not being allowed to meet the guests. Tarini was fast asleep in her room just a few feet away. No one had any inkling of the terrible tragedy that was about to befall.

8 December 2021
6.03 p.m.

A series of tweets put out by the Indian Air Force confirm what the country has been dreading, engulfing people in a wave of shock and disbelief:

Gen Bipin Rawat, Chief of Defence Staff (CDS) was on a visit to Defence Services Staff College, Wellington (Nilgiri Hills) to address the faculty and student officers of the Staff Course today. Around noon today, an IAF Mi 17 V5 helicopter with a crew of 4 members carrying the CDS and 9 other passengers met with a tragic accident near Coonoor, TN.

With deep regret, it has now been ascertained that Gen Bipin Rawat, Mrs Madhulika Rawat and 11 other persons on board have died in the unfortunate accident.

Gp Capt. Varun Singh SC, Directing Staff at DSSC with injuries is currently under treatment at Military Hospital, Wellington.

# Epilogue

On 8 December 2021, around 12.20 p.m., the Mi-17 helicopter carrying Chief of Defence Staff General Bipin Rawat, his wife, Madhulika Rawat, and twelve others crashed into a heavily wooded area of the Coonoor ghat in the Nilgiris, western Tamil Nadu, barely 10 km from its landing site. Visibility was said to be limited that day. Had everything gone well, the Mi-17 it would have landed at the Wellington Golf Club helipad in another seven minutes. Gen. Rawat was going to deliver a lecture at the Defence Services Staff College (DSSC), Wellington. According to media reports, the Mi-17 took off from the Sulur air base at 11.45 a.m. It lost contact with air traffic control around 12.08 p.m.

Shortly past 6 p.m., the Indian Air Force confirmed that General Rawat, his wife and ten others on board had died. The sole survivor at the crash site, Group Captain Varun Singh, who suffered severe burns, was initially treated at the Military Hospital, Wellington, and then taken to Command Hospital, Bangalore, where, despite all the efforts to save his life, he succumbed to his injuries on 15 December.

*The timeline for the helicopter crash has been taken from ABP News and* India Today *reports.*

# A Few Good Men

Twelve of our country's finest men in uniform lost their lives in the helicopter crash that took Gen. Bipin Rawat and Madhulika Rawat. They were the best in their field, which was why they were serving with the Chief of Defence Staff. Their demise was not just heartbreaking for their families but also a terrible loss for the nation.

## Brig. L.S. Lidder, SM, VSM

Brig. Lakhwinder Singh Lidder, or Toni, as he was affectionately called by friends and family, was Defence Assistant to the CDS. He was from 2 Jammu and Kashmir Rifles and spoke fluent Gorkhali, since his unit had two Gorkha companies. He had briefly served with Gen. Rawat in Congo and later hosted him and Mrs Rawat on a ten-day trip they had made to Kazakhstan, where Brig. Lidder was posted as Military Attaché. He had obviously made an impression since he was handpicked by Gen. Rawat for the post of Defence Adviser.

Brig. Lidder hailed from Panchkula, Haryana, and was a second-generation army officer. Besides being an exceptional officer, he was a loving husband and son, and a doting father, who had got his daughter's first book of poetry published in November 2021. He had been approved for his next rank and was to take over as General Officer Commanding of an army division. He is survived by his wife, Geetika, and sixteen-year-old daughter, Aashna.

## Lt Col Harjinder Singh

Col Harjinder Singh was born on 17 April 1978. His pet name was Monty. It had been given to him affectionately by his grandfather, a Major in the army, who was a fan of the legendary British Field Marshal Bernard Montgomery. Harjinder and his brother, Tejinder, were just twenty and sixteen, respectively, when their father, Col Abinder Singh, who was from the Corps of Engineers and posted in Delhi, succumbed to brain hemorrhage. Barely three months later, they lost their mother to pancreatitis. While Tejinder, who was then in the twelfth standard, went to Lucknow with his uncle to finish his schooling, Harjinder shifted to the Army Boys Hostel in Delhi, completed his graduation and then joined the Officers Training Academy, Chennai, from where he graduated and got commissioned into 2/11 Gorkha Rifles in September 2001. Tejinder subsequently joined the Corps of Engineers and is commanding a unit now.

While serving in Baisakhi, Arunachal Pradesh, with the 40 Infantry Brigade, Harjinder met Maj. Agnes Menezes, who happened to be posted there as Education Officer. The two of them fell in love and got married when posted together in the Indian Military Academy, Dehradun. Harjinder was under posting as Camp Commandant of the Uri Brigade, when he received a personal call from Gen. Bipin Rawat, asking him if he would like be Staff Officer to the CDS. Harjinder agreed, and his posting got diverted to Delhi. Harjinder had been picked up by the General since he had the reputation of being an honest and straightforward officer.

Col Harjinder was a sincere soldier, a devoted husband and a loving father to his daughter, Preet, who was just thirteen when he passed away.

## Naik Gursewak Singh

Naik Gursewak Singh, from 9 Para Special Forces, had been serving as Principal Staff Officer to Gen. Rawat for three years. Gursewak had joined the Indian Army in 2000 and was posted in Udhampur before being attached with Gen. Rawat three years ago. Most of his career years in the Army were spent in the frontier areas of Jammu and Kashmir, Ladakh and Poonch. He was a demolition specialist and an expert in unarmed combat and close-quarter battle.

Naik Gursewak was a native of Dode Sodhian village in Tarn Taran district and is survived by his wife, Jaspreet Kaur, two daughters aged nine and seven, and a three-year-old son.

## Naik Jitender Kumar

Naik Jitender Kumar, from 3 Para Special Forces, was Personal Staff Officer (PSO) to the CDS. He had enrolled in March 2011. He had served extensively in the desert sector along the Indo–Pak border, at the India–China border near Pithoragarh and in J&K. He was an expert sniper and a specialist in communications. He belonged to Dhamanda village in Sehore district, and is survived by his wife, his five-year-old daughter and two-year-old son.

## Lance Naik B. Sai Teja

Lance Naik B. Sai Teja, twenty-seven, was also PSO to the CDS and had enrolled in 2013. He belonged to 11 Para Special Forces and had served in high-altitude areas in Arunachal Pradesh, along the border with China. He had participated in counterterrorism operations in Manipur and Nagaland. An expert of mixed martial arts, unarmed combat, and communications and electronic warfare, Lance Naik Teja belonged to Eguva Regada village in Chittoor district of Andhra Pradesh. He came from a family of farmers. His brother, Mahesh, also serves in the Army. Teja is survived by his parents, wife and two children, aged one and three.

## Lance Naik Vivek Kumar

Lance Naik Vivek Kumar belonged to 1 Para Special Forces. He had enrolled in December 2012, and had served in south and north Kashmir, as well as ahead of Spiti, at a location near the India–China border. He was a communications expert, and a specialist in combat freefall and unarmed combat. Lance Naik Vivek came from Jaisinhpur in Kangra district of Himachal Pradesh. He was PSO to Gen. Rawat.

## Havildar Satpal Rai

Havildar Satpal Rai, forty, who came from Takdah, Darjeeling, was the Personal Security Officer of the CDS. He was from 5/11 Gorkha Rifles, same as Gen. Rawat, and had enrolled in March 2002. Hav. Rai had served in Siachen, Naushera, Nagaland and Manipur. He is survived by his wife, Mandira Rai, and his nineteen-year-old son, who, joined 5/11 GR a year back.

## Group Captain Varun Singh, SC

Gp Capt. Varun Singh belonged to a family of soldiers. He was posted at the Defence Services Staff College as Directing Staff. Singh's father, Colonel K.P. Singh (retd), served in Army Air Defence, while his brother, Lieutenant Commander Tanuj Singh, is an officer in the Indian Navy.

Gp Capt. Singh was awarded the Shaurya Chakra on Independence Day in 2021, for saving his light combat aircraft

(LCA) Tejas during an aerial emergency on 12 October 2020. When his aircraft was facing emergency issues and needed to be vacated, not only did Varun stay in his aircraft but also managed to land it safely, despite technical hitches, averting a crash. He was awarded the Shaurya Chakra by the President of India for this act of bravery. Singh's Shaurya Chakra citation says he showed a 'high order of professionalism, composure and quick decision making, even at risk to his life. He not only averted the loss of an LCA, but also safeguarded civilian property and population on the ground.'

Singh belonged to Deoria in eastern Uttar Pradesh. On 8 December, he was the sole survivor at the helicopter crash site. He was first treated at the military hospital in Wellington and later shifted to the Bengaluru Command Hospital. But he succumbed to his injuries on 15 December. The thirty-nine-year-old test pilot is survived by his wife, Gitanjali, and their two children—eleven-year-old son, Radduman, and eight-year-old daughter, Aradhya.

## Wing Commander Prithvi Singh Chauhan

Wing Commander Prithvi Singh Chauhan, forty-two, was an accomplished pilot serving as Commanding Officer of the 109 Helicopter Unit, based at Sulur. He was piloting the ill-fated Mi-17 V5 helicopter when it crashed. The only brother to four sisters, he was the youngest of five siblings. The family was originally based in Madhya Pradesh, where Prithvi attended school. In 2006, they moved to Agra, where Prithvi's father started a bakery business. Prithvi studied at the Sainik School in Rewa, Madhya Pradesh, and got selected for the National Defence Academy. He went on to join the Air Force Academy and got his commission on 22 June 2002. His old parents had been waiting for him to come home in January.

He is survived by his wife, Kamini, twelve-year-old daughter, Aradhya, and nine-year-old son, Aviraj.

## Squadron Leader Kuldeep Singh

Sqn Ldr Kuldeep Singh was the co-pilot of the helicopter. He belonged to Gharana Khurd, a small village in Rajasthan's Jhunjhunu district, and had joined the Indian Air Force as a helicopter pilot in June 2015. Sqn Ldr Singh studied at Kendriya Vidyalaya, Mumbai, and then went to St Xavier's College. He came from a defence family and wanted to join the Air Force. Sqn Ldr Kuldeep is survived by his wife. They had been married for just two years. She had been with him in Coimbatore, which was his last posting.

## Junior Warrant Officer Rana Pratap Das

A native of Talcher, Odisha, JWO Rana Pratap Das had enrolled in the Indian Air Force in June 2006 and had served for twelve years. He is survived by his wife and one-year-old son.

## Junior Warrant Officer Pradeep Arakkal

JWO Pradeep Arakkal was the chief engineer of the Mi-17 and had served in the Air Force for nineteen years. He belonged to Thrissur district in Kerala and had participated in many major operations taken on by the Air Force, including anti-Maoist missions in Chhattisgarh, and flood-rescue operations carried out during the 2018 deluge in Kerala. He is survived by his wife, seven-year-old son and two-year-old daughter.

# Acknowledgements

This book could not have been written if Col Satpal Parmar, the late General Bipin Rawat's mamaji, and Lt Gen Rakesh Sharma, his closest friend, had not guided me through my arduous journey as I tried to piece together his life from interviews with people who knew him best. Not only did both of them give me time and interviews, they also helped me with contacts and phone numbers, introduced me to people who might not have talked to me otherwise and patiently verified the information I was unsure about. It reached a point when, I suspect, they started dreading my phone calls and WhatsApp messages. Gen. Sharma, in fact, ribbed me that I should be sharing royalty with him since I was treating him like my research assistant. I thank them both from the bottom of my heart for their generosity.

I am grateful to Tarini for sharing with me the memories of her loving parents, and to Geetika Lidder for sharing the memories of her late husband, the caring Brig. Lakhbinder Singh Lidder, which helped me reconstruct that last day of their lives. To both of them, I apologize for making them relive the pain.

I thank all of Gen. Rawat's friends, family and comrades who agreed to be interviewed for this book (the number crossed twenty) and gave me insights into different phases of his life, sharing with me those heart-warming anecdotes that made him come alive as a person for me. I would also like to thank Col Jaishankar Singh, Commanding Officer, 5/11 Gorkha Rifles, and Lt Col Sachin Kamboj, Second-in-Command, for generously sharing old photographs of Gen. Rawat from their regimental albums, many of which you see in this book.

I am grateful to my St John's College, Agra, classmate Lt Col Anupam Gaur, from the Army Aviation Corps, who not only found me the pilot who had taken Gen. Rawat on the Dimapur chopper flight that had crashed—in which all on board had a miraculous escape—but also helped me reconstruct the two chopper flights mentioned in the book, particularly the unfortunate one from Sulur, which happened to be Gen. Rawat's last.

I am grateful to my Tamilian friend, the Bangalore-based Anitha Kumar, who interviewed the Tamil-speaking Nazar (the Coimbatore-based eyewitness of the Sulur chopper crash) and transcribed the interview in English for me; and to Lt Col Raju Pradhan, for writing the Nepali lines for me. And also to Palash Mankodi—the young, aspiring army officer, fellow Instagrammer friend and mixed marshal arts (MMA) expert—who helped me put together the boxing jargon for Gentleman Cadet Bipin Rawat's boxing scene.

I would like to thank Reshma Negi, first cousin of Gen. Rawat, and Kulbhushan Negi, her husband, for passionately insisting that I take up this biography in the months when I had started working on it but had not yet signed the Penguin contract, since I was unsure if I would be able to do justice to it.

In the end, I would like to thank my Penguin Random House editor Gurveen Chadha, for being my pillar of support; the brilliant Vineet Gill, for editing the book; Penguin design head, Ahlawat Gunjan, for coming up with the stunning concept for the cover and the back page (Gorkha hat representing the General's going away); and to Amit Srivastava, artist par excellence who has so beautifully managed to capture the spirit of the late General in the portrait you see on the cover. It was a dream team to work with, and I consider it a privilege to have had this opportunity.

Lastly, I am grateful to my brother, Col Sameer Bisht, for always reading every single chapter of every single book I have written, and for uncomplainingly coming back with feedback and suggestions, despite his busy schedule. He reposes faith in me as my late father once did, and that means more to me than anything else. And yes, of course, I am glad to have as my forever bouncing board my closest friend, my husband Col Manoj Rawat, who had to listen to every story of the General's life that touched me, before I sat down to write. Then, of course, Hukum, whom I thank for just being there and wagging his big tail for me from time to time. He won't be reading this and would probably prefer a bone.

Scan QR code to access the
Penguin Random House India website